THE
YEAR
I WAS
BORN

Compilers Frances Farrer
and Alison Graham

Signpost Books

Published by Signpost Books, Ltd
25 Eden Drive, Headington, Oxford OX3 OAB

First published 1994
10987654321

Based on an original idea by Sally Wood
Conceived, designed and produced by Signpost Books, Ltd
Copyright on the format Signpost Books, Ltd 1994
Compilers: Frances Farrer and Alison Graham
Designer: Paul Fry
Editor: Dorothy Wood

ISBN 1 874785 21 X

Acknowledgements: Mirror Group Newspapers plc, for all the pictures in which they hold copyright
and Tom Ashmore for his invaluable help in retrieving them from the files; The Worshipful Company
of Fishmongers and Camera Press for permission to reproduce the Annigoni portrait of Her Majesty
the Queen, p90, Hulton Deutsch Collection p68, Molly Blake for permission to reproduce the picture of her mother Annette Mills with Muffin the Mule, p6; National Motor Museum, Beaulieu, p68;
Range Pictures Ltd, p90.
Every effort had been made to trace all copyright holders, but if any have been inadvertently
overlooked, the publishers will be pleased to make the necessary arrangements
at the first opportunity

Printed and bound in Belgium by Proost Book Production

WINTER TAKES A CRUEL GRIP

WINTER'S icy grip: Women waiting for the sales to open in London faint with cold; roads in 52 counties are affected and power lines come down. But people rally round to help the elderly and infirm. For others, like these children in Wick (right) it's not all bad news . . .

Rindone in Detroit, USA, and knocks him out in the sixth round.

6 Thursday

After 14 hours of talks, the NUR suspend the **rail strike** due to start at midnight next Sunday. The British Transport Commission, headed by Sir Brian Robertson, agrees to investigate the recommendations of the

court of enquiry which had been set up to investigate the dispute.

7 Friday

Railmen are awarded a **pay rise** after suspending their threatened rail strike. The rise will benefit 60,000 men and the increases will be implemented next Monday.
■ Labour MPs Michael Foot and James

Callaghan refuse to take part in TV's In the News, after Director General Sir Ian Jacob bans any discussion of the rail strike threat. His decision sparks off one of the biggest ever mixups in the BBC's 28-year history as the panel of radio's Any Questions were discussing it on the Light programmel.

8 Saturday

Princess Margaret returns to London from Sandringham wearing the latest fashion—a swagger coat.
. . .ELVIS PRESLEY celebrates his 20th birthday, SHIRLEY BASSEY her 18th . . .

9 Sunday

12 million bushels of Canadian **wheat** is coming to Europe, mainly for Belgium and the UK.
■ **Marian Anderson** is acclaimed for her performance in A Masked Ball at the Metropolitan Opera House in New York. She is the first Negro singer to appear there in its 71-year history.

10 Monday

Plans are announced for a group of Commonwealth explorers led by Sir Edmund Hillary and Dr Vivian Fuchs to cross **Antarctica** in surface vehicles, in 1957, and set up two permanent bases for geophysical studies.

■ **Annette Mills**, creator with Anne Hogarth of the popular TV puppet **Muffin the Mule**, dies aged 60. She was the writer of many popular songs including Bumps-a-Daisy, and had also been a well-known ballroom dancer.
. . . Death of Horace Annesley Vachell, aged 93 in Bath. Britain's oldest novelist, he was working on his 101st book . . .

11 Tuesday

Following the announcement of the death of Annette Mills, the TV studios at Lime Grove are flooded with calls from children asking where they can send flowers.
■ Mrs T. White of the Dial Pub, Bocking, Braintree, Essex appealed for scraps of wool for knitting toys in the Daily Mirror in November 1954, and has ended up with 2000 boxes full. The tap room at the Dial is out of action while it is sorted.
■ Ford's Lincoln-Mercury division unveil an outstanding new car—the **Futura**—at the Chicago Motor Show. It is 19ft long, 7ft wide, and 52in high. No details of its performance have been released yet.

12 Wednesday

President Eisenhower asks Congress for the power to 'save Formosa from Chinese Communists.'
■ **Blizzard** maroons a train in 5ft drifts at Bower station, nr. Wick, Scotland. Ten men and two women have to spend the night on board. The station master's wife keeps them going with hot tea.

13 Thursday

Princess Margaret's chauffeur-driven Rolls Royce skids on ice near Baldock, Herts, hitting the car in front. The princess's police escort then crashes into the back of the Rolls. Fortunately no-one is hurt. Further blizzards sweep the south of England, causing a five-mile long traffic jam on the London-Oxford road at High Wycombe, after a succession of collisions.
■ The **Schoolboy's Exhibition** at the Royal Horticultural Hall, London closes after 12 days. Lost property includes 1,500 gloves (mostly right handed), 2,000 caps, a selection of satchels, diaries, hats and scarves.
. . . Born: Fred White, of Earth Wind & Fire . . .

14 Friday

Funeral service for Annette Mills at St Martins-in-the-Fields in Trafalgar Square.

THE HITS OF 1955

The Number One Hits (no Top Ten list was published at this time)

Jan 7	**Finger of Suspicion**	Dickie Valentine
Jan 14	**Mambo Italiano**	Rosemary Clooney
Jan 21	**Finger of Suspicion**	Dickie Valentine
Feb 4	**Mambo Italiano**	Rosemary Clooney
Feb 18	**Softly Softly**	Ruby Murray (below)
Mar 11	**Give Me Your Word**	Tennessee Ernie Ford
April 29	**Cherry Blossom Pink and Apple Blossom White**	Perez Prado
May 13	**Stranger in Paradise**	Tony Bennet
May 27	**Cherry Blossom Pink and Apple Blossom White**	Eddie Calvert
June 24	**Unchained Melody**	Jimmy Young (below)
July 15	**Dreamboat**	Alma Cogan (above right)
July 29	**Rose Marie**	Slim Whitman
Oct 14	**The Man from Laramie**	Jimmy Young (below)
Nov 11	**Hernando's Hideaway**	Johnstone Brothers
Nov 25	**Rock Around the Clock**	Bill Haley and his Comets
Dec 16	**The Christmas Alphabet**	Dickie Valentine

Source: New Musical Express

BLOCKBUSTER . . .

Rose Marie, Slim Whitman's recording of the 30 year-old love song, was No. 1 for 11 weeks, breaking all records for sustained chart success.

MOST POPULAR US BALLAD SINGERS

Johnnie Ray

Frankie Lane

Tony Bennet
(pictured, left)

Rosemary Clooney

Doris Day

Pat Boone

ROCK AROUND THE CLOCK

was recorded by **BILL HALEY (left) AND HIS COMETS in 1954,** but it was not until it was featured in the 1955 movie, *The Blackboard Jungle,* **that the record became a huge hit. Eventually it sold over a million copies in Britain alone and changed popular music forever.**

POPULAR BRITISH BALLAD SINGERS

Ruby Murray

Jimmy Young

Dickie Valentine
(pictured, right)

Malcolm Vaughan

David Whitfield

TERROR OF THE LONDON SMOG

JAN 16

'Black Pudding' **smog** in London. Blackness falls without warning just after 1pm. Terrified people pray or run screaming for shelter. Visibility is down to 2-3 yards. By 1.07 pm Central London is clear as the smog rolls back south, blacking out Wimbledon, Croydon, East Grinstead, and Tunbridge Wells. Half an hour later it blacks out Brighton, and then disappears out to sea. The weathermen say that a cloud of smog was trapped between a northerly and a south-easterly wind.

Floral tributes include a two-foot high Muffin the Mule.
■ **Petrol** price is increased by 5d. to 4s. 6d. a gallon

15 Saturday

SPORT: No racing today. The Wales v England **rugby** international is cancelled because of bad weather, as are many football matches.

■ More than 3,000 sheep are buried in snowdrifts up to 15ft deep in Ystradfelltle, a village near Brecon. The sea has **frozen** at Whitby, Yorkshire. and the Orkneys are cut off by the storms.

16 Sunday

A Vickers Viscount **aircraft crashes** at London Airport in thick fog. The pilot mistakenly taxies onto a disused runway, and the plane strikes a steel barrier at 80mph. All 30 aboard survive, but the pilot and one passenger are injured.

17 Monday

The world's first atomic-powered submarine sets sail today. She's the **USS Nautilus** (pictured). It weighs 3,000 tons, measures 300 ft and cost £18 million. She starts a week's trials in Long Island Sound, with a crew of 160 Navy and civilian experts on board.

18 Tuesday

Blizzards have buried whole communities in Scotland. Ships, planes and helicopters try to get food to villagers facing **starvation** in Caithness, Sutherland and the Orkneys. The aircraft carrier *Glory* has sailed to Lossiemouth to act as a floating airfield for helicopters. The ship's cooks are busy baking bread to be dropped. The BBC is broadcasting instructions to villagers to make big letters in the snow to help aircraft—D for doctor, F for food, C for cattle fodder, etc.
... RAILWAYMEN are to get the full three shillings in the pound pay rise they asked for before calling off the rail strike, backdated to January 10 ...
■ 'Sky shouting' planes fly low over the Kenya hills broadcasting a new call to the **Mau Mau terrorists** hiding in the forests to surrender. Sir Evelyn Baring, the Governor of Kenya, goes to the chiefs and elders of the Kikuyu tribe, from which Mau Mau sprang, to tell them of the offer.

19 Wednesday

The **killer smog** comes back to London as dusk falls. Early frost left a layer of cold, still air over the capital. Smoke from chimneys is trapped under the umbrella. London Airport closes down. Thousands of Londoners cough and gasp in the yellow-grey murk. Hospitals prepare for casualties suffering from breathing difficulties.

1955 FACT FILE

World Population	2,528,000,000 (est)
World's Largest City (in population)	London 8,224,163 (est).
	(8,346,137 in 1951 Census)
UK Population (males)	23,534,061
UK Population (females)	25,464,815
Total UK Population	49,574,300
	(48,998,876 in 1951 Census)
Total UK Area	89,034,2 square miles
Total London area	616.4 square miles

Head of State	Queen Elizabeth II
Prime Ministers:	1) Sir Winston Churchill
	resigned 5 April
	2) Sir Anthony Eden MP
	(pictured)

House of Commons
(After the General Election on May 26)
Conservatives 345 seats, Labour 277 seats, Liberals 6 seats ,
Sinn Fein 2 seats (declared invalid).

Astronomer Royal	Sir Harold Spencer Jones
Poet Laureate	John Edward Masefield (below)
Royal Swan Keeper	F T Turk

UK Statistics	
Births	786,500
Deaths	595,900
Marriages	410,600
Divorces	28,894
Licensed motor vehicles	6,260,173
TV licences	5,156,000

Emigration statistics	
to Australia	35,200
to Canada	27,800
to New Zealand	10,200
Total UK Emigration	102,900
Total UK Immigration	64,900

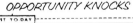

The Council of Europe
Belgium, Denmark, France, Irish Republic, Italy,
Luxembourg, The Netherlands, Norway, Sweden,
UK, Turkey, Greece, Iceland,
Saar, German Federal Republic.

Central Treaty Organisation
(pact of mutual defence): Turkey, Iraq, the UK, Pakistan and Iran.

NATO Countries
North Atlantic Treaty Organization: Belgium, Canada, Denmark,
Federal German Republic, France, Great Britain, Greece, Iceland,
Italy, Luxembourg, the Netherlands, Norway, Portugal, Turkey, USA

20 Thursday

The Society of Motor Manufacturers says that British car, lorry and bus production topped the million mark for the first time last year. Numbers were divided almost equally between home and export markets.

■ The beginnings of a **thaw** in the north of Scotland, which now faces a flood menace.

21 Friday

Coal prices up by 6d. a ton in the London area. Average grade now costs £6.11s.

■ Police in a busy station in Liverpool find the dog with a message tied to its collar saying, 'Please look after my dog. Mummy doesn't like it. — John.' The dog, now called Peggy, has a new home with one of the policemen who says 'John' can visit her whenever he likes.

■ Scientists confirm that **Piltdown Man** was a complete hoax.

22 Saturday

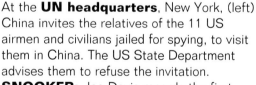

At the **UN headquarters**, New York, (left) China invites the relatives of the 11 US airmen and civilians jailed for spying, to visit them in China. The US State Department advises them to refuse the invitation.

SNOOKER: Joe Davis records the first official highest break of 147.

■ Paris **flood disaster**. The Seine is at its highest for 30yrs. 30,000 are homeless and 18 have died. Troops have been rushed to the city in case a mass evacuation is ordered. Hundreds of rats have fled the flooded sewers and taken refuge in nearby basements.

23 Sunday

Seventeen die and 43 are injured when an **express train jumps the rails** and

crashes into a platform at **Sutton Coldfield** station, nr. Birmingham. A packed express train coming in the other direction is stopped by a woman running along the line waving at it, and by the fireman and engineer of the **crashed train** who break into a signal box and set the signals to danger. The express stops only 200 yards from the wreck, six coaches overturn and many passengers are trapped. Sutton Coldfield station was locked, as it isn't used on Sundays.

■ **Well done, Sunbeam!** A Sunbeam Talbot, driven by Capt Per Malling and Gunnar Fadum of Norway wins the Monte Carlo rally. Seven of the first 12 places are taken by British cars. Sheila van Damm of London, also driving a Sunbeam, wins the women's cup is 11th overall.

24 Monday
New Moon

Sir John Rotherstein, director of the Tate Gallery, announces that Rodin's statue **The Kiss**, is being bought for the nation for £7,500.

■ **President Eisenhower** asks Congress

to support plans for helping the Chinese nationalists on Formosa under attack from Red China. It might involve attacking Red Chinese troops on the Chinese mainland. The Red Chinese Home Secretary, Hsieh Chueh-Trai, said his country hoped to take Formosa within a year.

■ Thieves raid the home of **Harold Macmillan**, the Defence Secretary, at Chelwood Gate, Sussex, and steal a large amount of silver. Thieves get in through a pantry window.

25 Tuesday

R A Butler, Chancellor the Exchequer, announces equal pay for women in the Civil Service, but pay will not be completely levelled out until 1961, as the increases will be made in seven equal yearly instalments.

■ British Rail says that, after 130 years of service, **steam trains** are redundant and will be replaced by cleaner, faster, diesel locomotives. It is part of a £1.2m plan to give Britain a better rail service and will take 15 years to complete.

. . .Russia formally ends its state of war with Germany . . .

■ First sighting of the **flying bedstead**— the experimental plane used for testing vertical take-off.

26 Wednesday

The motorboat *St George*, reported to be loaded with arms including hand-grenades, mines and dynamite, has been seized trying to sneak into a lonely cove on **Cyprus.** The British destroyer *The Comet*, escorts the motorboat into Paphos. Cyprus has suffered from riots stirred up by agitators who want union with Greece.

27 Thursday

50,000 **Communist soldiers** are reported to be massed on the Chinese mainland opposite the nationalist-held island of Marsu. More than 500 American and Chinese Nationalist war planes are within easy striking distance of China.

■ The **Bank Rate rises** ¹/₂% to 3¹/₂%.

28 Friday

CRICKET: The Fourth Test match begins in Adelaide, Australia. At 4pm the temperature had reached 102°F. The lowest temperature in the last two days has been 80°F at 6am.

■ Britain and New Zealand call for a meeting of the UN Security Council to try to end the **fighting** in the Chinese civil war.

■ Mr Jiggs, London Zoo's nine-year-old orang utan, is being put on a diet. He weighs a portly 17st 4lbs, and has a 47-inch waist and a 51-inch chest.

29 Saturday

Frank Howarth, a grocer from Blackburn, Lancs, is reducing the price of five commodities to help pensioners. They will be able to save 4d a lb on butter and bacon, 3d. on a 1/4lb of tea and cooked meats, and 1 1/2d on 2lbs of sugar. He feels sorry for the number of **pensioners** who look in his windows and pass by.

■The Cunard liner *Queen Mary*, on her way to Cherbourg, answers an SOS call by a Panamanian ship, *Liberator*, in the Atlantic. She takes 2 injured men on board. She is expected to dock in Cherbourg on Monday, only a few minutes behind schedule.

30 Sunday

Sir Edward Mellanby (70) dies. His research work led to the discovery of **Vitamin D**, and put an end to rickets, a bone disease that crippled thousands of under-nourished children.

■ Russia accuses the USA of **aggression** against Communist China, and asks for urgent consideration by the UN.

. . . The *Woman's Sunday Mirror*, **a new Sunday paper exclusively for women, makes its appearance, price 3d . . .**

■ It's 50°F in Blackpool. So many people go out for a

stroll on Hampstead Heath that traffic comes to a standstill.

31 Monday

Princess Margaret leaves for a month's tour of the Caribbean, her first official solo visit. She is seen off from London Airport by the Queen, the Duke of Edinburgh and the Queen Mother.
■ Nearly 400 people have volunteered to try to catch colds at the Common Cold Research Unit in Salisbury, in response to a Ministry of Health Appeal.

FEBRUARY
1 Tuesday

The Atomic Energy Commission assure Greville Howard MP that radioactive waste dumped 150 miles off Lands End is not dangerous.

2 Wednesday

The Church in Wales buys **Bush House** in the Aldwych, London, the headquarters of the BBC World Service, for £2.5million They say the income will help to increase the stipends of their ministers of £445 pa which compare unfavourably with English stipends of £550.

■ **CRICKET:** England win the Fourth Test in Adelaide by five wickets, and retain the Ashes.

3 Thursday

Britain will spend £147 million on roads, including a new motorway from London to Yorkshire. Traffic will have restricted access and there will be flyover crossings and junctions. (See panel, below)

4 Friday

Brigadier-General Sarnhoff of RCA in the USA announces the development of a **magnetic tape recorder** for television. The tape can be wiped clean and used again and again.
... The Hudson river freezes from shore to shore for the first time in 37 years ...
■ The civil war in China hots up. Prime minister **Chou En-Lai** urges the UN to drive out Chiang Kai-Shek and admit Communist China. Chiang threatens to invade China.

5 Saturday

Viscountess Boyle, known to million of TV viewers as **Katie Boyle** because of her appearances on 'What's My Line?', flies off to the West Indies. Her husband is suing for divorce, alleging desertion.
■ 11,689 dogs, groomed to within an inch of

GOVERNMENT GETS THE SHOW ON THE ROAD

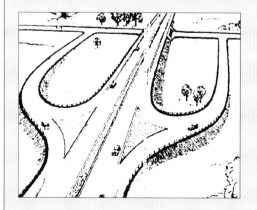

MOTORWAYS ARE HERE: The Government's four-year plan to modernize the British road system will get underway with a London to Yorkshire motorway, and another one from Birmingham to Preston. There are also plans to build bypasses around nine major cities including Doncaster and Maidenhead. There are many complaints that despite this massive investment in the road programme, there are no plans to build a motorway to the Channel ports, or a bridge across the River Severn.

■ Left, artist's impression of an innovative 'flyover'.

their lives, are on show at Crufts Dog Show, which opens today.

6 Sunday

Prima ballerina **Margot Fonteyn**, marries Panamanian diplomat Roberto Arias, in Paris, right.

■ The BBC is re-recording 8,000 sound effects so that they can be broadcast in VHF. The BBC sound effects library is thought to be the largest in the world. It contains 50 different version of a car starting and stopping.

7 Monday

Passengers on the train from King's Cross to Edinburgh complain about having to stand while dogs, some covered with satin sheets, sleep on the seats. The dogs are returning home from Cruft's Show.

■ In France, the government of M Pierre Mendes France falls after eight months in office, over French policy in North Africa.

■ About 1,000 pitches of about 10' x 8' in Chislehurst Caves, Kent, are to be let to the general public at £1 per annum for shelter in time of war.

8 Tuesday

The Commonwealth Prime Ministers Conference, meeting in London, accepts Pakistan's intention to become an independent republic within the Commonwealth.

... **M Pinay is asked to try to form a new French government.** ..

■ Stockton-on-Tees magistrates refuse to relax Sunday rules and allow the famous Italian opera star, Beniamino Gigli to sing at the Globe Theatre at 3pm on Sunday. Concerts are not allowed to start before 7.45 p.m. on Sundays so as not to interfere with churchgoing.

9 Wednesday

Georgi Malenkov resigns as premier of the Soviet Union to make way for Krushchev's candidate, Marshal Bulganin.

■ There was a slight rise in **unemployment** in Britain between December 6 and January 10 this year, to a total of 298,000.

... **Snow returns to southern England, with the temperature 27°F and falling** ...

■ The Rome underground, which has been talked about since 1881, and under construction since 1938, is officially opened.

10 Thursday

The **BBC** announces plans for the experimental transmission of **colour television** in 1956.

...**M Pinay's proposed French cabinet is rejected.**

■ The House of Commons defeats the proposal on the suspension of the **death penalty** for five years despite a moving speech by Chuter Ede MP who, as Home Secretary in 1950, refused to reprieve Timothy Evans. Evans was hanged for the infamous murders committed by John Christie at 10, Rillington Place, Notting Hill.

11 Friday

Safety belts will be an optional extra in new Ford cars. Ford have developed seat belts which they believe will help prevent head injuries. Front seat belts will cost 31s. plus 7s. for fitting. Rear belts will be 26s., plus 2s 6d. for fitting.

FEBRUARY

12 Saturday

The Reverend Athol Simpson of Mickley, Northumberland, says no one should put less than 7d. in the collection plate at church. At present, collections bring in only £140 a year, leaving the church with a £120 deficit.
■ M Pflimlin is asked to form a new French government.

13 Sunday

London bus and trolley services are to be cut because of the falling numbers of passengers. London Transport executives put it down to the rising number of private motorists, motorcyclists and the habit of watching television, which is cutting down the number of people who travel in the evening.

14 Monday
St VALENTINE'S DAY

The BBC is offering exclusive three-year contracts to variety stars and other personalities in an attempt to stop commercial television, which starts in September, acquiring their services. So far those who have said no to the BBC include Bernard Braden, Barbara Kelly, Benny Hill,

■ M Pflimlin fails to form a government in France.. . ..

15 Tuesday

The Government announces that it intends to build 12 **nuclear power** stations during the next 10 years at a cost of £300 million.
■ On show at the British furniture exhibition in London is a kitchen cabinet containing a built-in refrigerator, radio, bread bin, ironing board, clock, electric timer, linen box, and china cabinet. It will cost £65.
. . . M Pineau tries to form a new French government.
■ The head of BBC TV, Sir George Barnes, wants to restrict **commercial broadcasting** hours to five a day. He feels more would have a bad effect on the country's social life. The independent companies don't agree and are angling for breakfast, elevenses and lunchtime spots.

16 Wednesday

A bit of canvas that has patched a skylight in the Marchioness of Dufferin and Ava's castle nr Belfast has been identified as a painting by the 18th century French artist Boucher. It is worth £10,000.
■ The General Electric Company says it has discovered how to produce industrial quality **synthetic diamonds** by simulating temperature and pressures 240 miles below the surface of the earth.
■ M. Pineau who is trying to form a new French government, has offered the post of Vice-Premier to Pierre Mendes France. M France, who was himself overthrown just 11 days ago, is reluctant.

17 Thursday

The Government announces the historic decision to manufacture the **H-bomb**.
■ **Helen Keller** (74), the blind and deaf American who has done so much to help those similarly afflicted, holds a press conference in London. She answers the questions she receives via the manual

---

BBC-TV FAILS TO SIGN UP THE STARS . . .

Big guns opting out of the battle against commercial channel (from left): David Nixon, Jimmy Edwards and Peter Sellers

Bob Monkhouse, Frankie Howerd, David Nixon, Jimmy Edwards, Harry Secombe, Peter Sellers, Spike Milligan, Eric Sykes, Eamonn Andrews and Richard Dimbleby.

alphabet, clasping her companion's hand.
. . . Flashing INDICATORS on cars are under investigation, as there have been some protests that they are not as effective as the semaphore arm signal. . .
■ The Ministry of Works announce that no sheep will graze this year in Kensington Gardens, London, because of the large number of dogs around. They will continue to graze in Bushey and Richmond parks.

18 Friday

Thousands of listeners phone the BBC in tears on hearing of the death of Bo'sun the dog in 'Mrs. Dale's Diary'. Mrs Dale herself weeps on air, but Bo'sun's bark is just a recording.
■ Profirio Rubirosa, the much-married Dominican diplomat, seeks a divorce from his fourth wife, the Woolworth stores heiress **Barbara Hutton**, on the grounds of incompatability.

19 Saturday

Anthony Wedgwood-Benn (29), left, who wants to renounce his right to the title Viscount Stansgate, has been told by a House of Lords committee that his objections are not sufficient to allow him to bring in the necessary personal Parliamentary Bill.
. . . M Pineau fails to form a government in France.

20 Sunday

The worst **snow** for eight years covers the country from John o'Groats to Lands End. Farmers in the north of Scotland are afraid they may lose 12,000 sheep. A train that left Inverness on Friday, takes three days to reach Helmsdale, on the coast 80 miles away, due to the snow.
. . . P.C. Goldie (28), reports for work at 6 am at Blackpool police station, on skis and on time . . .

21 Monday

Road conditions in Britain are the worst for eight years. 30° of frost in Kew Gardens. The island of Foula in the Hebrides, has been cut off for seven weeks.
■ The **BBC** announces that it is to reduce its output of radio programmes as TV is proving more popular. When commercial television starts transmitting this autumn, radio's evening audience is expected to shrink further. BBC executives are considering merging the Home Service and the Light programme.

22 Tuesday
New Moon

A Technical Irradiation Group of 12 scientists receive a £50,000 research grant to discover uses for **atomic ash**. The team leader suggests that the ash might be used to strengthen clothing, to harden plastics for housebuilding and to sterilize drugs.
■ Princess Margaret causes a **sensation** when she appears at a state banquet, and then a charity ball at University College, in Kingston, Jamaica, with her hair clipped in a bun, like Queen Victoria, and wearing a strapless rose-pink slipper-satin gown with a foaming tulle bustle.

23 Wednesday

The selection committee at the Comédie Française in Paris ban George Bernard Shaw's play *Mrs Warren's Profession,* as they consider it to be amoral, boring, and unsuitable for presentation.
Edgar Faure becomes French Prime Minister again.

PREMIER-GO-ROUND IN FRANCE . . .

Musical chairs at the top in France, where M Pierre Mendes France (right) is overthrown and a succession of colleagues try unsuccessfully to form a government, (from left) M Pinay, M Faure and M Pfimlin

BOOKS OF THE YEAR

THERE is a bumper crop of bestsellers, including a title from someone not noted as a literary source — showjumper Pat Smythe (below, right). Kingsley Amis has further success with *Lucky Jim*, while Ian Fleming scores a hit with further adventures of James Bond.

Lucky Jim	Kingsley Amis
The New Men	C P Snow
Jump for Joy	Pat Smythe
Still Digging	Sir Mortimer Wheeler
Man of Everest	Sherpa Tensing
Kathleen Ferrier	edited by Neville Cardus
I'll Cry Tomorrow	Lillian Roth
Village School	Miss Reade
The Intelligent Heart	Harry T Moore
The Unknown PM	Robert Blake
The Wilder Shores of Love	Lesley Blanch
Don Camillo's Dilemma	Giovanni Guareschi
Coromandel	John Masters
Love of Seven Dolls	Paul Gallico
The Winds of Heaven	Monica Dickens
Moonraker	Ian Fleming
Adventures in the Skin Trade	Dylan Thomas
Bonjour Tristesse	Francoise Sagan
To Whom She Will	R Prawar Jhabvala
The Chrysalids	John Wyndham

24 Thursday

It will cost £7-£12 to adapt your TV set to receive the new **commercial television** programmes later this year. New aerials will cost from 7s. 6d. to 10s. Nearly a million TV sets will not be suitable for conversion. The London commercial television station will transmit from Croydon and will cover an area about 40 miles west (Henley), 35 miles north (Hertford) and rather less south and east.

■ **Lady Docker** wants to field a team of crack female marbles players in the Good Friday **Marbles** Championship at Tinsley Green, Sussex, despite the fact that the chairman of the British Marbles Board of Control tells her that under present rules women are not allowed to play.

BORN: Alain Prost, French world championonracing driver.

25 Friday

R A Butler, **Chancellor** of the Exchequer, announces new hire-purchase restrictions on cars, radios, television sets, furniture and household goods.

■ The **bank rate** is raised to 4 1/2%, its highest for 23 years.

■ **Albert Schweitzer** is awarded an honorary OM. The only other honorary OM still alive is President Eisenhower.

. . Christian Dior dominates the Paris shows with his new A-Line range . . .

■ The Queen takes a small party to Covent Garden to see Margot Fonteyn dance the title role in *The Fire Bird*. Opera House staff wear their royal blue livery with scarlet waistcoats for the first time since the War.

■ UN disarmament committee talks open in London.

■ LADY DOCKER

26 Saturday

Foundation Day, Australia

Up to £1,000 is being paid on the **black market** for invitations to the State Banquet in Nassau to be attended by Princess Margaret next week.

. . . 30 foot high snow drifts in the north . . .

CRICKET: The start of the Fifth Test Match in Sydney is postponed because of heavy rain.

27 Sunday

To improve the comfort of **racegoers,** Auteuil racecourse has installed central heating in the first five rows of the reserved stand and totaliser hall. Eventually they will heat the upper gallery and the public stands.

■ The Royal Australian Air Force drop food and medical supplies over 1,000 sq miles of New South Wales, when the Macquarie, Hunter and Namoi rivers all burst their banks.

28 Monday

The Norman crypt at Rochester Cathedral, Kent, is unveiled after extensive renovation.

■ Stephen Pigott (75), the man who designed the engines for both the *Queen Elizabeth* and the *Queen Mary* dies.

■ **King Hussein** of Jordan (19) announces his engagement to Egyptian princess Dina (25). She works as a Cairo university lecturer. They first met when both were studying in London.

. . . Striking busmen in Gillingham, Maidstone and Chatham, Kent, are refused service in shops, pubs and even taxis. . .

PRICE LIST	
TV Licence	£5
Radio Licence	£1
Road Tax	£12.9s
Income Tax (standard rate)	8s 6d
Dog Licence	7s 6d
Birth certificate	3s 9d
Marriage Certificate	3s 9d
Death certificate	3s 9d
Stamp (inland)	2½d
Stamp (overseas)	4d
Family Allowance (weekly)	8s per child
Old Age Pension	2s-26s

PRINCESS MARGARET TOURS THE CARIBBEAN

February 1955 sees **Princess Margaret**'s first official solo tour. She proves to be hugely popular throughout the islands of the Caribbean—with officials and the local inhabitants alike.

■ Israeli forces raid the Gaza strip in violation of the 1949 armistice, and kill 6 civilians and 36 soldiers.

MARCH

St DAVID'S DAY

1 Tuesday

TV aerials on the Tower of London have been removed as they are not considered to be in keeping with the character and dignity of their surroundings.

■ On a visit to the Magic Circle Club with his uncle, Admiral Earl Mountbatten of Burma, the **Duke of Edinburgh** saws his private secretary, Lt-Commander Michael Parker, in two. 120 magicians cheer the Duke. The Magic Circle is preparing a box of tricks for Prince Charles.

... The averge weekly earnings of male manual industrial workers over the age of 21 has risen above £10 for the first time.

■ Mr Macleod, Minister of Health, says that despite complaints that people were taking home the **wrong babies** because they were wrongly identified, the method of sewing marked tape around the wrists of babies to identify them in maternity hospitals will stay.

CRICKET: The Fifth Test Match in Sydney starts with sparkling batting from Tom Graveney and Peter May, who adds 182 runs in 160 mins.

2 Wednesday

Figures just issued show that there was a sharp decline in cinema attendance in the final quarter of last year. 12 million fewer people went to the **cinema** than in the same quarter of 1953. It is thought that this is because they are watching television instead. The cinema industry has decided to meet the challenge with brighter, wider screens and better and more entertaining films.

■ NYE BEVAN: pointing out flaws in Clement Attlee's H-bomb stance

■ **Aneurin Bevan**, MP, asks the leader of the Labour Party, Clement Attlee, to explain the Opposition's attitude to the use of the **H-bomb**.

3 Thursday

The ban imposed on Germany at the end of the War against **commercial flying** has been lifted. By May they will be flying passengers to European countries, and by June they will be crossing the Atlantic. British European Airways is to hand over about half its flights between London and Düsseldorf, which will involve them in a weekly drop in revenue of £5,500.

■ Australia's **floods** have killed 200 and left 44,000 homeless. It is estimated that the floods also killed 300,000 sheep in New South Wales.

■ A former RAF Warrant Officer, claims in the **divorce** court that the sandwiches his wife gave him to take to work were made with stale bread and filled with mud. He is granted a divorce on the grounds of cruelty.

■ TOM GRAVENEY: In sparkling form for England Down Under

4 Friday

Lady Docker's team become the All-England Women's Marbles Champions. She and her team play a match in Castleford, Yorkshire, against a team of factory workers. Lady Docker (17) is beaten by laundry girl Brenda Dyson, but the Docker team is better all-round.
■ From October 1, the City of London is to become a **smokeless** zone.
■ The Burnham Committee recommend that **equal pay** for women should be adopted by teachers.

5 Saturday

All UK aerodromes are to have their own **customs** facilities.
■ Boer War **veteran** Walter Kerr (80), waits for nine hours in a Metropolitan Line siding at Neasden before calling out to railwaymen to ask when the train will move. Walter was once a fellow prisoner of war with Winston Churchill.
■ **Dr Billy Graham** claims that 34,000 converts recorded 'decisions for Jesus', at his Harringay meetings last May.
. . . An excess of SEAWEED on the south coast is causing anxiety to Worthing and its neighbours. The last time they had this much seaweed, it was followed by a plague of flies.

6 Sunday

Between 10,000 and 25,000 Chinese in Singapore smoke **opium.** And now the British government is prohibiting its sale. Some Chinese temples offer cures in a week, starting with the sacrifice of a cockerel, and continuing with prayer and tea.
■ Preparations are completed for the building of foundations for a new Coventry Cathedral, designed by Basil Spence.

7 Monday

Princess Margaret marriage sensation. Will she decide to abdicate her right of succession to the throne and her £6,000 a year civil list allowance to marry **Group-Captain Peter Townsend** (40) as he is divorced? She will be 25 in August, and can marry without the Queen's consent.
■ The National Association of Schoolmasters is concerned that the **Burnham** Committee recommendation on equal pay for women teachers will lead to the decline of the man in the teaching profession.
■ Three more villages are **evacuated** in the path of boiling lava from the Kilauea **volcano,** Hawaii, which has been erupting for a week.1,000 acres of sugar cane has been devastated.
. . . A driver who crashed her car, and offered as defence that as she was asleep so she could not be held to have been driving it, is dismissed by Justices in the High Court.

8 Tuesday

The largest **atomic device** yet tested is set off at dawn in the Nevada desert. The mushroom cloud rises to 40,000 feet, and lights the sky over southern California, 250 miles away, and is visible over the Black Hills of Dakota, more than 800 miles away.
■ Opposition leader **Clement Attlee** (Labour, pictured) says war must be abolished and calls for a reduction in arms.

NUCLEAR DEBATE TO THE FORE

POWER OF THE BOMB:
Crowds, equipped with
sunglasses against the
glare, witness an A-Bomb
test in Nevada. An
awesome sight with
equally awesome results
(sequence, left), as the
shock waves rip apart a
test-site building.

■ Thousands pack the City of London as **Princess Margaret** arrives for 'welcome home' lunch after her Caribbean tour.

9 Wednesday

A conference of some of the most influential Jewish organizations in the United States urges the American government to make a determined effort to bring Israel and the Arab states together in direct **negotiations** for a peace settlement.

■ War minister Anthony Head says that the **National Service** call-up must stay at two years. It is the only way of keeping the Army up to size.

10 Thursday

Television is to be allowed in the lounge bars—though not the public bars—of Glasgow public houses. But the television sets must not be operated for the final 15 mins before closing time.

RACING: Gay Donald, ridden by Tony Grantham wins the **Cheltenham Gold Cup** by ten lengths.

11 Friday

Snub-nosed girls and jug-eared boys are bringing a boom to **plastic surgeons**. The National Health Service pays for children who are distressed by teasing to have plastic surgery. Adults must prove their health is adversely affected before the NHS will pay for their plastic surgery, and there are 10,000 on the waiting list.

■ The Granada **cinema** chain is asking its patrons to vote on whether the National Anthem should be played at the beginning of a performance, the end, or not at all. This is to avoid the undignified rush for the exits which often takes place.

■ The House of Lords is in favour of the creation of **life peers**. It is even suggested that women should be admitted.

■ The death is announced of **Sir Alexander Fleming** (74), the Nobel Prize winner who invented penicillin (left).

12 Saturday

American jazz musician, **Charlie 'Bird' Parke**r, dies.

■ John Betjemen wins the William Foyle £250 poetry prize for *A Few Late Chrysanthemums*.

■ The great east window of **Bath Abbey**, destroyed by bomb blast in 1942, will be unveiled tomorrow. About half the glass, in fragments, was saved.

13 Sunday

The 5th RAC British Rally ends in Hastings. The winners are J H Ray and B Horrocks, driving a modified Standard 10 saloon, and Miss **Sheila van Damm** (right) and Mrs A. Hall in a Sunbeam. The navigation tests in the narrow lanes of Wales, Yorkshire and elsewhere make the British rally virtually impossible for foreign competitors to win.

14 Monday

Six hundred **Archers** fans pack the church at Hanbury, Worcs. when Phil Archer finally marries Grace Fairbrother. Fans cars jam the church drive and hold up the recording van for half an hour, Police reinforcements have to be drafted in to control the traffic. The producer wanted the wedding recorded in a church to capture the right atmosphere. Officially the 10 million Archers' fans will not hear about the 'wedding' until Easter.

15 Tuesday

Two 15-year-old boys wait 60 hours outside a Glasgow shop to buy £60 motorcycle for just 2s. 6d. The proprietor promised the motorcycle to the first customer today to offer him a half-crown minted in 1947.

■ One minute's **advertising** on London's commercial television station will cost £1,000, says the Associated Broadcasting Company. Birmingham rates will be about half this as there are fewer viewers.

16 Wednesday

The Parliamentary Labour Party decides by a majority of 29 to withdraw the party whip from Mr Aneurin Bevan because of his attitude during the defence debate. He counter-attacks people who accuse him of manoeuvres against Mr Attlee's leadership.

■ Secret documents from the **Yalta** Conference of 1945 between Mr Churchill, President Roosevelt and Marshal Stalin reveal Roosevelt's proposal that Britain should return Hong Kong to China.

. . . The government announce that the ROYAL MINT is to be rebuilt. It will be situated at 1-31 East Smithfield. The present Royal Mint was completed in 1811. . .

■ From next winter BBC-TV and the ITV companies will not broadcast between 6-7pm on weekdays and 6.00-7.30pm on Sundays so that small children can be put to bed before the evening's viewing begins. All programmes will end at 11pm.

■ BLUEBIRD: US think it might make a weapon

HEAR Billy Graham

CLIFF BARROWS and choir of 1000 VOICES

GEORGE BEVERLY SHEA
WORLD RENOWNED GOSPEL SINGER

KELVIN HALL, GLASGOW

MARCH 21 to APRIL 30

NIGHTLY at 730
SATURDAYS 4 and 730
NO SUNDAY SERVICES

THIS SPACE IS DONATED BY DAVID ALLEN & SONS LTD

ALL SEATS FREE
ALL SCOTLAND CRUSADE 1955

PRAISE BE!

MARCH 18 Hymn-singing shopgirls give Billy Graham a film star's welcome at Plymouth. The American evangelist is here for a four-month crusade in Britain and on the continent, starting at Glasgow's Kelvin Hall next week.

17 Thursday
ST PATRICK'S DAY

The Royal Fine Art Commission is considering a 'boulevard' scheme to reconstruct Hyde Park Corner, London and set the Wellington Arch in an area of grass.
■ The US Navy think that Donald Campbell's **Bluebird** turbo-jet speedboat

could form the basis of a wonderful war weapon. Mr Campbell says he is prepared to let them have it if they want it for the defence of the free world.

18 Friday

Heather Jenner, whose **marriage bureau** has arranged more than 5,000 marriges, is being sued for divorce by her husband, landowner Michael Cox. He cites Stephen 'Lifemanship' Potter as co-respondent.

19 Saturday

The Epsom Derby authorities reject the BBC's offer of £1,500 to televise the race, so it will not be shown on television this year. **The Derby** used to be shown on television before the war.
■ Weather update: 15ins of snow in Wick.

20 Sunday

Television is being accused of causing such conditions as **illiteracy,** stooping shoulders and a disease called TV neck. And now it has been blamed for keeping people out of public houses.
■ In the USSR, they are celebrating the 130th anniversary of the birth of **Alexander Mozhaisky,** the scientist who 'invented the aeroplane and heavier-than-air flight'. It is claimed that he invented a flying projectile first tested in St Petersburg in the summer of 1882.

21 Monday

Teachers blame mothers who go out to work and leave the shopping for children to do, for an inundation of 'sick leave' notes. They also blame the cinema for luring children away from school and the NHS, which allows children with trivial complaints to visit the doctor!
■ Mongrel **dogs** have had their day, according to dog experts. Improved standards of living have turned people into 'dog snobs'. Nowadays dogs are better looked after, and don't wander the streets mating indiscriminately.

22 Tuesday

Brixton is in the news as Councillor N H White, Mayor of Lambeth, exposes landlord **racketeering.** Poor housing with short leases is all black people can get. He gives as an example a nine-room house with no bathroom on a 10-year lease that was sold for £750 to a West Indian. It wouldn't fetch

half that sum any other way, he says, as no building society would lend on it.
■ A new edition of the **Highway Code** is published.

23 Wednesday

The Postmaster General reports that the rate of **telephone** connection has increased from 355,000pa in 1951 to 410,000pa in 1954.
■ One of the BBC's top announcers, **Macdonald Hobley** (38), has rejected an offer from commercial television because he wants to broaden his range. He is considering starring alongside Viscountess (Katie) Boyle in a domestic comedy series instead.
■ Farmer Goodall of Rossington, Yorkshire, is thinking of claiming compensation from the Air Ministry, after a jet plane breaking the **sound barrier** causes his prize porker, Polly, to give birth to eight piglets a week early. They all die. His champion peke also gives birth a week early, and three of the five puppies die.

Got the map?

Got the SPANGLES?

Mmm! How delicious! And Spangles give you a 'lift' just when you need it. Get some to-day!

Five wonderful varieties — FRUIT FLAVOUR · MINT
BARLEY SUGAR · ACID DROP
BUTTERSCOTCH

Fruit flavour SPANGLES
Fruit flavour SPANGLES

Life's always sweeter with SPANGLES · 3d.

Amalgamated Engineering and Electrical Trades Unions are asking for another 58s.6d. per week. The only paper of national stature to continue publishing is the *Manchester Guardian..*

... Lancashire mills announce extended Easter holidays, because of the shortage of orders.

■ Cambridge win the 101st **Boat Race** by 16 lengths in 19mins 10secs. They also beat Oxford at chess, 4-3.

■ QUARE TIMES, owned by Mrs W Welman, wins the **Grand National** at Aintree.

27 Sunday

A sealion that escaped from Chester Zoo finds a happy home in the garden of Mr A Halliwell of Long Lane, Chester. Sonny (10 months) swims in the 8ft pond in Mr. Halliwell's garden and catches the fish with which it is stocked.

24 Thursday
New Moon

Aneurin Bevan is saved from expulsion from the Labour Party by one vote and the intervention of Clement Attlee.

■ Lord Beveridge criticizes the government for refusing to subsidise home helps, while providing support for the tobacco industry.

28 Monday

The dowager Lady Lloyd George and Lady Churchill are in the Peeresses Gallery in the House of Commons to hear Sir Winston announce that a monument to Lord Lloyd George will be erected. The House, and the ladies, are shaken by the appearance of a Lloyd George double in the Strangers' Gallery. The resemblance is uncanny.

■ California sends New York the first coast-to-coast colour TV programme in the USA.

25 Friday

A strike by 800 maintenance engineers stops all national daily and Sunday **newspapers.**

■ A divorce judge advises husbands not to flirt with their wives' friends. Mrs Violet Littler claims her husband, Ralph Littler, kissed the bare shoulder of the girl with whom he was dancing. Mr Littler says his wife put glass in his sandwiches. The case is dismissed.

29 Tuesday

Dockers are striking at three ports over men who have left the TGWU to join the National Amalgamated Stevedores and Dockers. 88 ships are affected, and it is thought the strike could move to London.

■ The Board of Trade is sending investigators to Hong Kong to look into the glove industry. English hand-made fabric gloves cost from 12s. a pair, while those made in Hong Kong start at 3s.9d.

26 Saturday

Newspaper strike: members of the

WHAT'S ON AT THE THEATRE

Waiting For Godot is given its first performance—to a mixed reception—and otherwise you can see Michael Redgrave and Diane Cilento in *Tiger at the Gates*; Wilfred Hyde-White, Celia Johnson and Anna Massey in *The Reluctant Debutante*; **Norman Wisdon** in *Painting The Town*; John Neville and Virginia McKenna in *Richard II*; Rex Harrison and wife Lilli Palmer in *Bell, Book and Candle*, and Alfred Drake and Doretta Morrow in *Kismet*. Dorothy Tutin scores a hit in *The Lark* with Leo McKern, as does Edmund Hockridge in *Can Can*.

THE BAD SEED	Malcolm Keen, Bernard Bresslaw, Diana Wynyards, Miriam Karlin, Joan Sanderson
TIGER AT THE GATES	Michael Redgrave, Diane Cilento
THE RELUCTANT DEBUTANTE	Wilfried Hyde White, Celia Johnson, Anna Massey
CAN CAN	Edmund Hockridge
WAITING FOR GODOT	Hugh Burden, Peter Woodthorpe, Peter Bull, Timothy Bateson
MOBY DICK	Orson Wells, Patrick McGoohan, Gordon Jackson, Joan Plowright
THE LARK	Leo McKern, Dorothy Tutin
RICHARD II	John Neville, Laurence Hardy, Virginia McKenna
MUCH ADO ABOUT NOTHING	John Gielgud, Moira Lister, Claire Bloom, Helen Cherry
PAINTING THE TOWN	Norman Wisdom
BELL, BOOK AND CANDLE	Rex Harrison, Lilli Palmer, Athene Seyler
KISMET	Doretta Morrow, Alfred Drake

Clockwise (this page, from top): Hugh Burden in Waiting for Godot; Rex Harrison and Lilli Palmer, Wilfrid Hyde-White, Celia Johnson, Virginia McKenna, Joan Plowright and (right) Athene Seyler. Facing page, anti-clockwise from top): Norman Wisdom, Alfred Drake and Doretta Morrow in *Kismet*, Dorothy Tutin, Michael Redgrave, Diane Cilento and Claire Bloom.

30 Wednesday

Two French trains share the world railway speed record, each of them reaching 206mph just south of Bordeaux.
■ Gloucestershire, parts of the Midlands, the Trent Valley and the town of Doncaster are fighting the floods. Hurricane Bertha strikes the South Queensland, Australia, coast causing widespread floods. Hundreds of families flee their homes.
■ Marlon Brando and Grace Kelly win Oscars for Best Actor and Actress in *On The Waterfront* and *Country Girl*.

31 Thursday

Prime Minister Winston Churchill is ready to **resign,** but will delay the announcement until the newspaper strike is over. This, in turn, delays the announcement of the general election, which will be made by his successor.
■ Drivers of lawn-mowers on public highways do not have to pass a driving test. Mowers are not treated as motor vehicles as they do not have horns, mirrors or lights.

1 APRIL Friday

The palace of Herod the Great, ruler of Judea in 40-4 BC, is discovered at Masada. Its authenticity is attested by the Israeli Department of Antiquities.
■ The financial year ends with a surplus of £433 million. Income tax receipts are £92 million over estimate.
■ Joseph Pulitzer, son of the Hungarian immigrant founder of the prestigious **Pulitzer Prize** for excellence in journalism, literature and music, dies. His father bought the St Louis Post Dispatch in 1878, and his son, Joseph, worked hard to maintain the paper as the guardian of the people's rights and the critic of their chauvinism.
■ Seven million workers in the mining, quarrying, building, gas, electricity, water, transport and communications industries now average £9.2s.3d. per week.

APRIL 5 WINSTON CHURCHILL leaves No. 10 for the last time as Prime Minister. His staff applaud him as he heads off to retirement. At the end of the road, hundreds wait to catch a glimpse of the great man.

2 Saturday

Tolls on the roads into East Germany are massively increased. The West say that the East's justification that it is to maintain their roads, is inadequate.
. . . A court of enquiry is set up to investigate the newspaper strike. . .
■ VETERAN: Francis Henry Edge (78), dies at home in Derbyshire. He claimed he was the youngest soldier at the relief of **Ladysmith** during the Boer War, in which he served in the King's Royal Rifles.

3 Sunday

Representatives from eight footballing nations meeting in Paris, set up a **European Cup** (above) contest.

CHURCHILL RESIGNS!

■ Over 300 people die when a train plunges into a canyon near the city of Guadalajara, Mexico.
Savings for the year 1954-1955 totalled £1,289,500,000 - the highest since the savings movement was started.

4 Monday

Mr N Dodds MP (Labour), asks the Minister of Food if he will ban the colouring of kippers with coal tar, and encourage a return to smoking the fish instead of painting them.
■ The Queen and the Duke of Edinburgh dine with Sir Winston Churchill at No 10 Downing Street.
■ A NHS patient has complained at having to pay 3s. for three **prescriptions** for chloromycetin for different members of his family. He thinks all three should have been on one form, saving 2s. The chemist replies

that the man received £21.10s.-worth of medicine.
■ Rochdale Corporation bus driver C Taylor celebrates the end of the trolley bus service in Manchester by taking 40 guests on a farewell trolley bus tour from Sale Moor to Hardy Lane.

5 Tuesday

Sir Winston **Churchill resigns.** The Queen arrives at Buckingham Palace at 4.22pm, followed 10 mins later by Sir Winston. The audience lasts 35 mins. A large crowd cheers Sir Winston as he leaves the palace.
■ Singer **Gracie Fields**, the down-to-earth Lancashire lass who became an international superstar, cancels her appearance at this year's Royal Variety Show, because of ill health following an operation in New York.

Exchequer; Selwyn Lloyd, Minister of Defence; Lord Home, Commonwealth Relations; Reginald Maudling, Minister of Supply.

MOTOR SPORT: John Surtees (21), Britain's motor-cycling superstar, wins three trophies, and sets three track records.

JOHN SURTEES: winning style

6 Wednesday

Sir Winston Churchill leaves No. 10 Downing Street, for his home, Chartwell, in Kent, for the last time. He has a Union Jack rug over his knees and his budgerigar, Toby, in a cage at his feet. Rufus, his poodle, follows in a second car.
■ **Sir Anthony Eden** becomes Prime Minister.

7 Thursday
Full Moon

The US senate approves the admittance of West Germany to NATO.
■ Councillor Simon Mahon of Bootle, Lancs, thinks there would be fewer mistakes made if all girls took their boyfriends home, so Bootle Housing Committee is building houses with a living-room and parlour where younger members of the family can do their homework—and later their courting.
■ Theda Bara (Theodosia Goodman), the silent movie star, dies.

8 Friday
Good Friday

Sir Anthony Eden names his **Cabinet**. The new line-up is: **Harold Macmillan**, Foreign Secretary, right; R A Butler, Chancellor of the

9 Saturday

The Liverpool Philharmonic Orchestra, under Sir Adrian Boult, gives the first performance in this country of **Shostakovitch's** 10th Symphony, in the presence of the Soviet Ambassador, Mr Jacob Malik.
■ The British Board of Film Censors express concern about **Marlon Brando's** film, *The Wild One*, as they fear it might titillate rather than reform juvenile delinquents.

10 Sunday
Easter Day

The **bad weather** fails to deter motorists from visiting the seaside, though railway stations are quiet. A spokesman for the railways suggests that people prefer to travel by car in bad weather as they can then sit in it on arrival. Hotels and hostels in Snowdonia and the Lake District are full.

11 Monday
Bank Holiday.

The busiest Easter Monday on the roads since the first traffic census was taken. Cars return to London at the rate of 3,000 an hour. There are traffic jams up to seven miles long on roads from Blackpool and Lancaster to Preston.
■ The remains of the Temple of Mithras on the Roman Wall at Carrawburgh, Northumberland, which was discovered by amateur archaeologists, are now open to the public. The original altars and pedestals have been moved to Durham University.

12 Tuesday

It is announced that **Jonas E. Salk**, (right) of Pittsburgh University, has successfully developed a vaccine against polio.

■ The president of the National Hairdressers' Federation Conference meeting in Brighton urges the women of the country to go to war against the long-haired, couldn't-care-less attitude that too many men in Britain still hold. The conference votes by 141 votes to 23 to charge a minimum of 2s. for cutting men's hair.

■ The death is announced of Fr Teilhard de Chardin (74), French palaeologist and orientalist. A world-class scholar, he was also geological adviser to the Chinese.

■ DR JONAS SALK: Polio vaccine

13 Wednesday

The Board of Survey of Canals and Inland Waterways recommends that one third, mostly in the Midlands and Lancashire, are closed, though they should be retained for use in the supply of water and for the drainage of effluent.

. . . Book borrowing from libraries has increased significantly during the newspaper strike, but so far there has been no great increase in book sales . . .

14 Thursday

In his address to the annual conference of the Royal Astronomical Society, Mr C Wood says that he thinks the journey to the moon and back will be achieved within 30-35 years. 10,000 Americans have already booked their seats for the round trip, and one man has staked his claim to all lunar fish-and-chip restaurants.

■ There is a fear of a **black market** in the Salk polio vaccine in America, though the public is assured of adequate supplies within the year. The World Health Organization warns that polio is not yet beaten, and the advantage of vaccinated over non-vaccinated children appears to be only 3.5-1.

15 Friday

Stalemate on the proposed talks between France, Britain and the US over South Vietnam. The French distrust Vietnam's **President Diem**, but the Americans support him. The British, who played an important part at the Geneva Conference in 1954, feel entitled to be at the talks, but the Americans don't want Britain there as they suspect that we agree with the French.

■ Author and playwright J B Priestley, speaking at the formation of the Cheltenham Literary Festival, says the Edinburgh Festival is too big and that one should be able to meet people at festivals.

16 Saturday

Hugh Gaitskell MP says that the **General Election** has been called for May 26, not because we have a new prime minister, but because the Government is afraid that last year's trade figures will get worse.

. . . Today is the anniversary of the battle of Culloden in 1746 . . .

17 Sunday
Summer time begins at 2am.

About 10,000 people attend the first ever National Motor **Coach Rally** to see 81 motor coaches, including one double-decker.

DEATH OF A GENIUS

APRIL 18

Albert Einstein (76), the renowned mathematical physicist and propounder of the Theory of Relativity, dies of arterio-sclerosis.

The coaches come from as far away as Cornwall, Manchester and the Isle of Wight. They have to drive at an average speed of 22mph to Clacton-on-Sea and then perform elaborate manoeuvres.

18 Monday

More **new companies** are being set up than at any time since the early post-war years, and the rate of failure amongst established firms is at its lowest for six years.

19 Tuesday

The newspapers will be back soon! The newspaper proprietors' original wage offer is accepted, pending negotiations to be completed within three months.
■ Chancellor of the Exchequer, R A Butler, in a pre-election budget, reduces the standard rate of **income tax** by 6d. in the £ and increases various other allowances.

20 Wednesday

Princess Dina Abdel Hamid (25) marries **King Hussein** of Jordan (19) at a ceremony at which, in accordance with Moslem custom, she is not present. Her father, Prince Abdul Hamid, signs the marriage contract on her behalf. The King attends an all-male reception at the palace, and the Queen has her own reception later. The new Queen's dress, made in Italy, costs £2,000.
■ Thomas Gerald Bolitho of St Martin's Lane, London, accused of stealing the first Strasbourg edition of *The Marseillaise* from the British Museum, says he stole it because he wants to go to Canada and has no money. He is sentenced to 21 months in prison.
. . . A Mau Mau gang murders two schoolboys on the outskirts of Nairobi. . .

21 Thursday

The **Queen's birthday.** She is 29 today.
■ Newspapers are published in London for

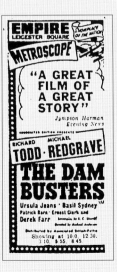

ACTION! BEST OF THE FLICKS

On the silver screen (clockwise, from top left): Jane Powell and Howard Keel among the Seven Brides for Seven Brothers; Marilyn Monroe in Seven-Year Itch, James Dean in Giant, Glenn Ford in Blackboard Jungle and, left, Richard Todd in The Dambusters and John Mills in The Colditz Story.

The Seven Samurai
Desiree
A Man Called Peter
Rififi
Daddy Longlegs
The Deep Blue Sea
Seven Brides for Seven Brothers
Bad Day at Black Rock
The Dam Busters
The Colditz Story
The Blackboard Jungle
The Man from Laramie
Children of Hiroshima
Dragnet
The Bridges of Toko Ri
Doctor at Sea
Carmen Jones
20,000 Leagues under the Sea
The Country Girl
The Conquest of Space
Geordie
The Seven-Year Itch
Lady and the Tramp
A Star is Born
The Ladykillers

the first time since March 25.

■ Blonde model **Ruth Ellis** (right) appears in court charged with the **murder** of crack racing driver David Blakely, who was found shot dead outside a Hampstead public house on Easter Sunday.

■ Dr Jonas Salk's new **polio vaccine**, which he tested on members of his own family, is to come to Britain. Polio claims nearly 3,000 lives a year in Britain.

■ After an 18-month investigation by the BMA, NHS doctors are given permission to use **hypnotism** on conditions such as deep-seated worries, stammering, facial twitches, severe headaches and insomnia.

■ Daisy Franks, left, becomes the first Women's **World Cycling Champion** at Herne Hill whem she returns 38.4secs for the 500m Flying Start a day after women's world records were officially recognised.

22 Friday
New Moon

A total of only seven broadcasts is planned to cover the first ever TV election. The press feel this should be doubled, as TV is the new political tool and people will no longer squeeze into church halls or stand on draughty street corners for a big political meeting.

SPORT: Britain's champion table tennis player, **Johnny Leach** (33), scores an impressive win over Yosio Tomita, the world Number 6, in Utrecht last night, and could be on his way to winning his third world title.

■ Anne Seymour (20), of Nottingham, dyes poodles pink, blue or green to match the outfits of their owners. She uses harmless vegetable dyes at her poodle parlour, and she says the animals love it. Her **doggie fashion** hint to owners—a dark green costume goes with a light green dog.

23 Saturday
St GEORGE'S DAY

A bronze plaque has been set in the pavement behind the statue of Charles I at the top of Whitehall to mark the point from which distances from London are measured.

FOOTBALL: Chelsea beat Sheffield Wednesday 3-0 to win the Football League.

■ Teenage heart-throb crooner Johnnie Ray opens his third season at the London Palladium to a rapturous reception.

24 Sunday

The South African cricket team arrives in London for the forthcoming Test series.

■ Lady Stair's house in Edinburgh is to be a children's museum sponsored by Edinburgh Corporation who own the building, and will be open in time for the Edinburgh Festival.

■ Official drought in southern England, Wales and parts of NW England where no rain has fallen for 15-17 days.

25 Monday

Actors are demanding more money for TV shows, and feel they should be paid in proportion to the number of people they entertain. A meeting of **Equity,** the actors' union, also resolves to disapprove of any Equity member being obliged to appear before any audience from which people are excluded on grounds of religion, politics, race or colour.

■ Lady Megan Lloyd George, a former Liberal and one of the finest women debaters ever to sit in Parliament, is to join the Labour Party. She is distressed by the Liberals' drift to the right.

26 Tuesday

The new Salk polio **vaccine** is to be tested on children and Manchester University students. All tests will be completed by the autumn. The vaccine is made from the kidneys of dead monkeys, and scientists fear a monkey shortage.

BOXING: Randolph Turpin knocks out Alex Buxton in the second round to win the British Light-Heavyweight title.

27 Wednesday

Commerical **televison** has signed up Gracie Fields, Bob Hope, Norman Wisdom, and Richard 'Mr Pastry' Hearne for lavish programmes each weekend. The shows will also be offered to the Birmingham and Manchester next year.

■ The new **Rolls Royce** Silver Cloud has a switch on the steering column to change the springing according to the state of the road, and a revolutionary new ignition key.

RACING: Our Babu beats Tamerlane by a neck to win the 2000 Guineas at Newmarket.

28 Thursday

It is the golden jubilee of the Automobile Association. From a membership of 90 in 1905, the AA has grown to 1,570,872 members. It was originally formed to warn members of police speed traps.

■ Unemployment figures for the quarter are the lowest for this period since the war. Unfilled jobs rose by 19,000.

■ Labour's General Election **Manifesto** pledges Labour will end the 11-Plus examination, help families who wish to buy their own homes, and establish an alternative public-service TV station which must be free from advertising. They will not bring back the ration book. The period of National Service will be reviewed, and they propose to end all H-bomb testing.

29 Friday

The BBC demonstrates VHF broadcasting,

■ OPEN FOR BUSINESS: The Duke and Duchess of Bedford with their family at Woburn Abbey, Bedfordshire.

which produces a remarkable improvement in fidelity and quality and cuts out whistles, buzzing noises and unwanted foreign voices.

■ The Tory General Election Manifesto is launched. The three main points are plans to make Britain a land of property owners, a promise to rehouse 200,000 **slum-dwellers** a year, and a promise to provide 1 million more school places, mainly in secondary schools, in five years.

30 Saturday

Woburn Abbey, home of the Dukes of Bedford for 400 years, is open to the public for the first time. His Grace the Duke of Bedford is on hand to collect the first half-crowns from the paying public.

■ Plans for travelling during the threatened

STIRLING SILVER—MOSS REIGNS SUPREME

Stirling Moss makes a great start to May by becoming the first Englishman to win the famous Mille Miglia. He drives a silver 3-litre Mercedes-Benz into Brescia in a record-breaking 10hrs 7min 48secs after leaving this morning. His average speed was 97.95mph.

rail strike include the running of special trains with non-striking staff; fleets of lorries and motor coaches for local distribution, and the display in private car windscreens of stickers with the RAC monogram and the word 'lifts'. Getting milk supplies to the big cities is a major problem.

MAY
1 Sunday

Arthur Deakin, the much-admired general secretary of the TGWU, collapses and dies while making a May Day speech at the Corn Exchange, Leicester.

2 Monday

Prospective Welsh Nationalist **candidate** for Gower, Edward Christopher Rees (24), is sentenced to 12 months in gaol for failing to attend a **National Service** medical.
■ The Ministry of Health is worried at the lack of candidates for training as **dentists.**
■ Nurseryman Leslie Green (42) is applying for public assistance. **Test jets** from Boscombe Down airfield are breaking the sound barrier, and his glasshouses, are ruining his business. Three weeks ago, splintered glass ruined 28,000 lettuces.
■ 26,500 Doncaster miners from 11 pits strike in support of the 2,600 men on strike at Armthorpe over a piece-rate dispute.

3 Tuesday

Theatrical producer Hughie Green, in the High Court, alleges that his BBC show *Opportunity Knocks* was taken off the air and replaced by the Carroll Levis show *Spot The Winner*, through the undue influence of Cecil Frank Meehan, assistant head of the BBC Variety department, whom Mr Levis, his wife Mina, or his brother Cyril had bribed.

■ The announcement by Sir Anthony Eden in the House of Commons that **purchase tax** will be taken off non-woollen cloth and domestic textiles is greeted with almost hysterical excitement. Parliamentary seats in Lancashire are in danger if the cotton industry doesn't get more help.

4 Wednesday

Mr Boyd-Carpenter, Minister of Transport and Civil Aviation, defends **parking meters** saying they ease congestion and raise funds for local authorities to provide off-street parking.

■ A **national survey** published in New York reveals that only one in 10 American wives goes through her husbands' clothes to see that all his buttons are on. And if a man demands a cup of coffee at some odd hour, only one wife in 20 will get it.

"AH, I SEE SALVADOR DALI'S IN TOWN AGAIN!"

5 Thursday

Speaking at the Newspaper Press Fund dinner, the **Duke of Edinburgh** confesses that during the strike he really only missed the strip cartoons.

■ The largest in a series of nuclear bomb tests in the Nevada desert creates such a shock wave that it is felt in Los Angeles.

... **The Occupation forces relinquish control in West Germany..** . . .

■ F W Woolworth & Co buy the **Adelphi Theatre** in the Strand, with the intention of turning it into a shop, but the London County Council will not permit alterations.

BORN: Hazel O'Connor - actress singer and songwriter.

6 Friday

Full Moon

Colin Cowdrey, the Kent and England cricketer, starts his national service in the RAF today, at Cardington, Beds.

. . . Parliament is dissolved.. .

MOVIES: Britain's favourite film stars are Marlon Brando and Jane Wyman followed by Rock Hudson, Humphrey Bogart and Audrey Hepburn.

7 Saturday

44 children get **polio** following vaccination with the new Salk vaccine, and the US government holds up further supplies. Surgeon-General Leonard Scheele says up to six million people have been vaccinated so far without ill effect.

■ Dozens of **bobbysoxers** scream, sob and swoon as heart-throb singer **Johnnie Ray** leaves London after his tour. Snack-bar girls leave their counters and rush towards the singer trying to kiss him. When his plane takes off they organise a sob session in the car park.

■ The number of miners on strike now totals 87,000. Seventy-two pits are closed.

FANS MOB SINGING STAR AT EVERY TURN DU

FOOTBALL: **Newcastle United** win the FA Cup for the fifth time in their history, beating Manchester City 3-1.

8 Sunday

The National Trust pays £6,000 for 111 acres (and a cottage) of Gatton Park Estate, once the property of Sir Jeremiah Colman of the mustard family. It already owns 108 acres of woodland there.

■ **An elk,** which wanders into the city, runs wild in Stockholm streets for two hours. The Flying Squad, pedestrians and children try to capture her until, exhausted, she jumps into a lake and tries to swim away. A fireman rescues her, vets sedate her then release her into the woods.

9 Monday

Actor and Producer **Orson Welles** (40) marries Paoli Mori (24), Italian actress and countess at Caxton Hall,

G HIS NATIONAL TOUR

WE LOVE YOU, JOHNNIE!

LOST IN THE CROWD: Johnnie Ray, a sell-out at every venue he plays, obliges fans outside the Palladium in London (left). His fans cross all age barriers, but the younger devotees wear their hearts on their sleeve—and Johnnie's name on their tops and his photograph wherever they can find a space . . .

London, at 8.40am. He says it happened so quickly he didn't have time to brush his hair. Welles (right) has been married twice before, most recently to Rita Hayworth.

10 Tuesday

The tulips in the parks of Lubeck, Germany, have a hole punched in one petal to discourage thieves.

■ Barbers in Ripley, Derbs, are charging an extra 6d. for special gentlemen's styles like the 'Boston crewcut' or the 'Piccadilly fringe', because they take longer to do.

11 Wednesday

The Queen's secretary, Cmdr Richard Colville, asks that as the **Queen** and the Duke of Edinburgh have decided that a certain amount of the Duke of Cornwall's education should take place outside his home and with other children, he should be allowed to visit museums, etc. without the embarrassment of constant Press attention.

■ Dr John W. Bell, a Harley Street specialist, says that expectant **mothers** should never drive cars as when they are pregnant they do things without knowing, and aren't safe on the road.

12 Thursday

The British Women's Pilots Association is formed today.

■ Vyvyan Beresford Holland (68), son of the playwright, poet and aesthete Oscar Wilde, is declared **bankrupt.** Holland is described as an author and journalist, and has worked as a sub-editor for the BBC. He admits to receiving large royalties from his father's works, and spending them immediately.

■ Canon Charles Raven, the Queen's chaplain, attacks the leaders of the Church of England for their unrelenting attitude to **divorce.** He agrees that marriage vows should not be broken, but feels that anyone tricked into marriage and then deserted is put into a difficult position by the Church when they find true love.

"I can't even raise a whisper till I've had my

WELGAR SHREDDED WHEAT"

Early morning apathy melts instantly as you enjoy delicious Welgar Shredded Wheat. This tasty rich-protein whole wheat breakfast is crammed full of energy-food in its most appetising and easily-digestible form —and you get the wonderful health benefits of wheat germ and bran. It's a treat that all the family will enjoy every day.

Buy the Big-Value Packet only 1/-

also available in the 'Small Family' packet 1d.

13 Friday

Jubilant Tories celebrate the results of the **borough elections** in England and Wales which produce a swing to the right. Labour lose 11 councils.

■ The new metal and plastics technologies are being applied in hospitals, especially orthopaedics, where replacement parts of the skeleton will become possible.

14 Saturday

The Eastern Bloc nations sign the Warsaw Pact.

■ The Pakistani prime minister, Mohammed Ali, has angered the 40,000 members of the League for **Women's Rights** by marrying a second wife. Many feminists have already thrown off the veil and called for complete equality of the sexes.

■ 18,000 **emigrants** have to wait to leave the country for Australia when a walk-off by 80 waiters stops the sailing of the 27,000 ton liner Georgic from Liverpool.

... Storms, hail, snow, heavy frost and sunshine all hit Britain today in a day of weather madness.

15 Sunday

Local authorities in South Wales and the West of England are trying to decide whether to underwrite an £11 million scheme to build a **bridge** over the River Severn.

■ About 10,000 people attend **Dr Billy Graham**'s first open air Industrial Rally at Dagenham Central Park, and about 200 answer Dr Graham's appeal. Accommodation for over 100,000 had been arranged by Ford Motor Company's Christian Fellowship Group. Ford supply him with cars and chauffeurs for his British campaign.

16 Monday

The fourteenth and final explosion of the 1955 series of **atomic tests** is set off in the Nevada Desert at 5am. The blast is more than twice as powerful as either Hiroshima or Nagasaki.

... The Yorkshire pit strike ends.

BOXING: Rocky Marciano (USA) retains his world Heavyweight title against Don Cockell, the British and Empire champion, when the referee stops the fight in the ninth round.

■ SNOW IN MAY! 5ins fall in Saddleworth, W Yorkshire.

17 Tuesday

Lt Col C E Howard-Vyse of Langton, N Yorkshire, objects so strongly to the look of four new red brick council houses among the mellowed stone cottages, that he gets his man to plant Virginia creeper around them. When the **tenants** complain about their damaged bulbs and flowers, he admits that he probably annoyed someone.

ROCK FALL: A rare sight as Rocky Marciano hits the canvas in his 1952 fight with Jersey Joe Walcott. But in May 1955, he still ruled the world, stopping Britain's Don Cockell in the ninth round.

■ The Scottish Church Commission recommends that women should preach and take part in the conduct of public worship.

18 Wednesday

White Rags the pony is saved from the slaughter house by a timely bid by 70 children from the Golden Horseshoe riding club of Sponden, nr Derby. Mrs Doreen Tunnicliffe puts her hand up with 18gns-worth of saved pocket money, whist-drive and concert proceeds. The only other bidder is the knacker's yard.
■ The first of the 60 Vickers **Viscount** airscrew-turbine airliners bought by the American domestic operator Capital Airlines is handed over today.

19 Thursday

The **first Wimpy Bar** opens in London .
■ Workmen are digging the foundations for the north block of County Hall on the south bank of the river Thames, London, and farther along test borings are being taken for Shell Petroleum's offices on the former Festival of Britain site.

20 Friday

The British Medical Journal calculates that several million doses of heroin are prescribed annually, but only about 40 **addicts** are known to the authorities. Motions from six different parts of the country protest to the BMA against the Government ban on heroin.

■ The liner **Queen Mary** leaves Southampton this morning after a 24hr turn-round—one of the fastest she has ever made at Southampton.
■ The Kenya government announce the break-down of talks with Mau Mau leaders for mass surrender.
... **DOCK talks are held at Downing Street.** ...

21 Saturday
New Moon

Frederick Ashton's ballet Romeo and Juliet, to music by Sergei Prokofiev, is given its first performance by the Royal Danish **Ballet** at the Royal Theatre, Copenhagen in the presence of King Frederick and Queen Ingrid.
■ Dame Lilian Barker (81), governor of the Borstal Institute for Girls, Aylesbury, Bucks, dies while on holiday in Devon.
GOLF: Britain's men go down 10-2 as the USA retains the Walker Cup .

22 Sunday

Billy Graham preaches to the **Queen** in her private Chapel at Royal Lodge, Windsor. After lunch the Queen thanks him for a 'fine, inspiring sermon'.

23 Monday

Dock **Strike.** 18,000 men are out at London, Merseyside, Manchester and Hull.
■ Ernest Edward Cook, who died in March, the grandson of Thomas Cook founder of the travel company, leaves his **art collection** to the National Art Collection Fund. It is the most valuable bequest they have ever had.

24 Tuesday

British **motor** manufacturers have broken all **records** during the first four months of this year. More than 400,000 cars, trucks and buses have come off the production lines for delivery in almost equal numbers to home and overseas buyers.

■ 30% of American boys and girls go to **college** at 18, according to the annual report of the Carnegie Foundation, against only 5% in Britain.

25 Wednesday

The 2,000-year-old **Grauballe Man**, one of Denmark's most famous archaeological discoveries, is being exhibited for the first time in Copenhagen. The skin on the hands is so fine that the police have been able to take fingerprints
■ Mme Leon Volterra's Phil Drake (100-8) wins the **Derby (above)** for France beating Panaslipper by 1 1/2 lengths.
■The assault party of the British expedition to Kangchenjunga, led by Charles Evans, reaches the summit, stopping 5ft below the actual summit to respect religious feelings of the Sikkhimese.

26 Thursday
ELECTION DAY

The **Tories** are re-elected with an overall majority of 59—Conservatives 344 seats; Labour 277 seats; Liberals 6 seats; Others 3 seats. It was a quiet poll.
■ Many scientists and engineers are leaving the UK for the USA and Canada. More than 20 firms are currently recruiting in the UK. Salaries offered range from £1,400-£4,280.

ELECTION SATIRE BY VICKY (AGED 98)

"YOUR HUSBAND NEEDS COMPLETE REST AND QUIET— HOW ABOUT TAKING HIM TO A FEW ELECTION MEETINGS."

ELECTION FEVER: a huge crowd gathers in Piccadilly Circus to await results. But it's not so arresting for one youngster!

27 Friday

As 740 West Indians land at Plymouth to search for jobs, they pass 20 returning to Jamaica, beaten by Britain's weather.
■ Young farm workers will be paid the full hourly rate from the age of 20 instead of 21, in an effort to get them to return to the land after National Service, rather than heading for the nearest factory.
SOFTLY, SOFTLY: Tenants in a large block of flats in Düsseldorf, Germany, have been asked by the landlord to wear slippers after 10pm to avoid disturbing their neighbours.

28 Saturday

The Rail Strike begins. The railways are almost at a standstill.
■ Actress **Hedy Lamarr** (41) offers to take a lie-detector test concerning a £17,850 jewel theft from her home, but she is so upset that the three attempts made are 'inconclusive', according to Houston, Texas, police.

29 Sunday

Railway **strike.** 65,000 railmen go on strike over pay differentials. Only 200 main line trains are running. All special Whitsun traffic stopped.
SPORT: Juan Fangio (Br) and Stirling Moss (GB) driving Mercedes Benz, finish 1st and 2nd in the production sports car race at the Nuerburg Ring, with 1/2 a length between them.

30 Monday
Whit Monday

The great trek home. Thousands of Whit holiday makers, lured to the coast by glorious sunshine, gamble on the rail strike not happening and today face the problem of getting home. Police stations become travel offices as they send out appeals to **motorists** returning from the seaside with spare seats to fill them with stranded travellers. It is the busiest-ever Whit Monday on the roads.

31 Tuesday

There is a skeleton rail service throughout the UK as 8,489 train drivers and firemen turn up for work: 41,532 stay away.
■ Announcing five new emergency regulations, the Government say that food supplies are safe, and motorists are asked to give lifts when possible. Third party insurance formalities for private cars are modified to allow passengers to be picked up, as long as the car is insured.
■ The United States Supreme Court rules that the southern states must end segregation in schools as soon as possible.

■ HEDY LAMARR: Lie test offer

43

FASHION HIGHLI

■ BIRTHDAY GIRL: Marilyn Monroe, who is 29 on June 1. Later she is seen out on the town with ex-husband Joe DiMaggio

JUNE
1 Wednesday

The train strike causes traffic jams all round London. Airlines schedule extra flights between London and Glasgow. The TUC summon the footplate men's leaders to a meeting.
■ Crooner **Eddie Fisher** (26) and actress **Debbie Reynolds** (23) deny reports that their engagement has been broken off.
. . . Marilyn Monroe is 29 today. . .

ITS OF 1955

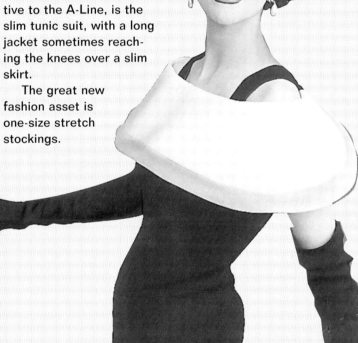

THE big Paris fashion story this spring is Christan Dior's A-Line, (illustrated, main picture, left). The dresses are flattish chested, but with an easy waist and a pyramid-shaped skirt.

The belt can be placed anywhere between mid hip and just under the bust, and skirts are just below the knee. The almost universal alternative to the A-Line, is the slim tunic suit, with a long jacket sometimes reaching the knees over a slim skirt.

The great new fashion asset is one-size stretch stockings.

2 Thursday

Grimsby **fish merchants** are using lorries instead of trains for their deliveries, saving thousands of pounds a day on delivery charges. Some say they will continue to send their fish by road when the strike is over.
■ BBC radio producers scoured Birmingham for an 11 year-old girl with a clear voice and two painful tonsils to star in a new **radio series** for Children's Hour—The Story of an Operation. Linda Walker has already made

the first recording, her tonsils are coming out today, and on Friday she will record the next programme.
■ FANCY THAT!: Peter Barker (29) and Anthony Newbank (28), both of Amesbury, bought a steamroller in Cornwall and, as it couldn't be delivered because of the rail strike, they decided to save the £52.10s. delivery charge and drive it the 150 miles home. On the way through Okehampton, Devon, the steamroller, belching smoke and sparks, set light to the thatched roof of a cottage, and within 30mins the house was a ruin. The cost of the damage was £4,500.

3 Friday

The Independent Television Authority lays down the guidelines for **television advertising**—it must be clean, honest and truthful; not contain any statement intended to promote sales by unfair comparison with competitive products; and the word 'guarantee' is to be used with caution, and sparingly.
■ Hugh Dalton, MP (67), announces that he will not stand for re-election to the Labour Shadow Cabinet. He urges Mr Attlee, in the interests of the Party, to select a much younger Shadow Cabinet and hopes that a number of his fellow veterans will follow his example.

4 Saturday

Sir Alexander Korda signs a contract with a US company that has patented Phonevision, a new system of **subscription television**. A non-scrambling number sequence is given to the subscriber to watch a particular programme.
■ 20,000 members of the Amalgamated Engineering Union are urged to stop repairs on locomotives and rolling stock to put greater bite into the **strike** by the 67,000 footplate men. 1,150 police reinforcements are coming from the provinces to help with traffic duty in London. Some factories have given their workforce notice as the rail strike is preventing production.

45

5 Sunday
Full Moon

Two out of five feature films made in Britain are now in colour—an 18% increase on 1953. ■ Marilyn Monroe and Joe DiMaggio, who were divorced last October, were seen together at the opening of her latest film, **The Seven-Year Itch**, in New York last week. Joe DiMaggio is said to be trying to win her back.

. . . The Prime Minister, Anthony Eden, broadcasts a personal progress report on the rail strike at 9pm. . .

6 Monday

500 British emigrants aboard the strike-bound Cunard liner *Ascania* at Liverpool threaten to **strike** as well when they are told to go ashore. One of the passengers, Mrs Doreen Ashton, who set out with her nine children nearly a week ago to join her husband in Canada, says, 'We have nowhere to go, and cannot afford to stay in this country now.' **CRICKET:** Peter May (left) is to captain **England** in the First Test against South Africa.

7 Tuesday

A report given to the annual meeting of the American Medical Association says heavy **smoking** increases the risks of cancer of the larynx, and heavy drinking may enhance the effect.
■ Eton College is investigating the disappearance of 10 gold coins the size of farthings and dating from Roman times, which have gone missing from the college museum. CID officers are quizzing housemasters, but the boys are not being interviewed. Each coin is worth less than £10.

8 Wednesday

A 60mph **tornado,** a boiling cone of mist over 1,000 ft high, rages over Dunstable and Luton, Beds, before disappearing back into the clouds. The only damage is leaves ripped from trees. By the time the tornado reaches built-up areas, it is 100 ft above the ground.

9 Thursday

In the Queen's **Birthday Honours list** published today, Dr Roger Bannister (26), the first man to run the four-minute mile becomes a CBE, and Sir Alexander Bustamante, former Chief Minister of Jamaica, becomes a knight, as does William Steward (54), Tory MP for Woolwich West, the first man for many years to make the House of Commons catering pay (he reported a profit of £425 after only three years).
■ Mr William Whiteley (72), Labour's Chief Whip, decides to give up his post when faced with a revolt by a large number of the younger MPs
■ B Hewson breaks the English native record of 2 mins 56.8secs for the 3/4 mile set up by Roger Bannister in 1951, with a new time of 2mins 55.4secs.

. . . The Duke of Cornwall and Princess Anne fly back to London from Balmoral - their first flight. . .

10 Friday

The **Duke of Edinburgh** (left) is 34 today.
■ Mr Clement Attlee is to remain leader of

the Parliamentary Labour Party with no time limit fixed for his going, after Mr Bevan implores him to stay.
■ The Metropolitan **police** are to patrol their beats by motor cycle in selected areas as an experiment. The Chief Commissioner says that a single policeman will be able to patrol a much longer beat than is possible on foot or pedal cycles.

11 Saturday

Disaster at the **Le Mans** 24-hour road race. (Full details on facing page). Britain's Mike Hawthorn driving a Jaguar wins the race. The French Cabinet has suspended all motor racing until new rules are formulated.

. . . All racing at Ascot is postponed because of the rail strike. . .

DISASTERS OF 1955

FANS FLEE as debris from three crashed cars devastates the crowd at LE MANS. Afterwards, one if the survivors surveys the horrific scene, barely able to comprehend it and, below, the stricken submarine SIDON disappears beneath the waves in Portland Harbour.

The **Le Mans 24 Hour Race** in June is the scene of the worst accident in motor-racing history, when three cars crash at speeds of 150mph and plough into the spectator's stand. **82 people are killed** and a further **73 injured**.

For 60 yards the sandy ground on one side of the eight-mile track is drenched in blood. Despite the carnage, the organisers decide that the race should continue, and Mike Hawthorne driving a Jaguar is declared the eventual winner. There were a record-breaking 250,000 spectators at the track to see the mass start turn to tragedy.

■ Britain suffers one of its worst peace-time naval tragedies when a practice **torpedo explodes** on the **submarine Sidon** as it is about to leave Portland Harbour, Dorset. As work is going on the submarine starts sinking. 13 crewmen are killed.

12 Sunday

One million copies of The Highway Code for Schools are to be distributed free.
■ The Post Office announce that they will now accept 1 1/2lb packages. Since the beginning of the rail strike they have only accepted packages weighing up to 8ozs.
■ The Queen, who was to invest Sir Anthony Eden as a Knight of the Garter, has postponed the ceremony for this year.

13 Monday

The rail strike has now been on for 16 days. **Peace talks** started last Wednesday, but there is still deadlock. The strike is costing British Rail about £5 million a week.
BORN: Tony Knowles, snooker player.

14 Tuesday

The Government gives the go-ahead to the construction of six more nuclear reactors—four at Windscale and two at Calder Hall.
■ The **rail strike** is off. The British Transport commission say that the restoration of suburban and residential transport must be a priority to get people back to work.

15 Wednesday

A **prisoner** serving 10 years in Colchester Prison for safe blowing leads the police and a bomb disposal squad to his cache of gelignite and detonators in Epping Forest, buried near a swimming pool.
■ The National Association of Master Bakers asks the government to grant an immediate increase in the price of the 14oz **national loaf** to 4 1/2d.

16 Thursday

The Government have dropped their

FORD POPULAR

£275

PLUS P.T. £115·14·3

Ford '5-STAR' MOTORING

 THE BEST AT LOWEST COST

WE MET A MAN THE OTHER DAY *who runs an expensive car—he can well afford to. He was driving a Ford Popular.* "It's my sister's" he said, " —and, since she won't let me keep it, I'll just have to get one for myself. It's the cheapest-running and most companionable car I've ever found. I dodge about town in it. I've been down to Devon and back. Seats four large men in roomy comfort. Must be the finest car value in the world. Only Ford could do it at the price."

(AND FORD SERVICE, TOO!)

proposals for compulsory **vehicle testing** for roadworthiness, but a Lords amendment seeks to strengthen the law forbidding the sale or supply of unroadworthy vehicles.
■ The **Queen Mary** is unable to sail, because 500 crew walk out on strike. Meanwhile, in New York, the Queen Elizabeth achieves her fastest-ever turnaround in 17hrs 9mins, knocking 34mins off her previous best.

17 Friday

The Admiralty announced late last night that there was no hope for the three officers and 10 ratings aboard the submarine Sidon when it sank in Portland Harbour, Dorset, yesterday. (See Disasters, page 47).

18 Saturday

The jewels which film star **Hedy Lamarr** reported stolen last month have been found, says oil millionaire Howard Lee, Hedy's fifth husband. Police say the jewels were found in a bag on the shelf in the sewing-room of the Lee home. It is the second time Miss Lamarr has reported the loss of jewels. In 1950, she reported that gems worth £50,000 had been stolen from her New York hotel bedroom. But tax collectors refused to allow a deduction she claimed for the stolen gems.

19 Sunday

Emperor Bao Dai of **Vietnam** is dismissed as chief of state by a 'council of the imperial family', and M Ngo Dinh Diem is nominated president of the Republic.
■ Harperley Station, Co.Durham, which was closed to passengers two years ago, took £1 from goods traffic last year and cost £132 to maintain. The station is to be closed.

20 Monday
New Moon

Len Hutton (left) is out of Test cricket for the rest of this year, for health reasons, and he may give up the game for good. Hutton will be 39 on Thursday, the first day of the Second Test.
■ Wimbledon Lawn Tennis Tournament opens today. For the first time since 1939, Britain has a female contender for the title in Angela Mortimer, winner of the French Championship two weeks ago.
■ The **wedding** of Australian tennis stars **Lew Hoad** and Jennifer Staley in Wimbledon on Saturday causes problems for the Australian Lawn Tennis Association, as official members of the party cannot have their wives with them on tours overseas.

21 Tuesday

Ruth Ellis (28), is found **guilty** of the murder of her racing-driver lover, David Blakely, outside a Hampstead pub in April, and sentenced to death.
■ **Sir Winston Churchill** is present at the unveiling of a bronze statue of himself in the Guildhall.

22 Wednesday
Longest Day

Chocolate War: the National Union of Retail Confectioners say that the Big Five—Cadbury, Nestlé, Fry, Terry and Rowntree— make too much profit, so they are refusing to display goods from these companies, and will boycott Cadbury products during July.
■ **Ruth Ellis** has decided **not to appeal** against the sentence passed on her yesterday. Now only a reprieve from the Home Secretary can save her.

23 Thursday

562 British day excursionists—the first 'no passport' trippers for 16 years—visit Boulogne. The Mayor cracks open some bottles of good French wine at a reception to celebrate. The adult fare from Eastbourne or Newhaven is 38s.6d.

■ South African batsmen face fiery **Fred Trueman** (left) for the first time in the Second Test Match that starts at Lords today.

24 Friday

Midsummer Day

More men than women are suffering industrial **accidents** caused by long hair says the Birmingham Industrial Safety Group.
South Africa start the day with a first innings score of 147 for 6, having blasted England out for 132 in their first innings.
. . . The QUEEN and the DUKE OF EDINBURGH receive a great welcome from the Norwegians as they arrive in Oslo on an official visit. . .

25 Saturday

French drinks containing less than 1% **alcohol** are to carry a tricolour stamp and the message 'Ministry of Public Health and Population approved'. The Minister of Public Health says that for some years young people have been drinking less and less alcohol, and he wants to encourage the trend.
■ **Pan Am** say that one of their airliners crossed from Prestwick, Scotland, to New York, USA, in 10hrs 9mins, beating by 25mins the record set by a BOAC airliner on June 2.

26 Sunday

Fifty-four passengers aboard a Spanish Airlines four-engined airliner sit with blankets wrapped round their heads and their shoes off as the plane comes in to land at London Airport. One of the tyres had burst as the plane was taking off at Madrid and, as it sweeps over the runway at Heathrow, the burst tyre drops off. The plane lands safely.

RUTH ELLIS —THE LAST

Ruth Ellis (28), ex-factory worker, waitress, dance band singer, photographic model, night club hostess and mother of two children, with her lover David Blakely (24).
Also pictured is the Magdala pub in Hampstead, where Ellis—the last woman to be hanged in Britain— shot Blakely.

JUNE

MAN HANGED IN BRITAIN

27 Monday

Norman Dodds, Labour MP for Erith and Crayford, says that he has a long list of **sportsmen** who have so far dodged **National Service**. 'There seems to be one law for the athlete and another for the not-so-athletic,' he says.

■ The Vicar of St John's, Sparkhill, Birmingham, wants the Church to prepare a list of **Christian names** for children from which parents must choose. He says that during the war-time desert campaign he was asked to christen children Tripoli, Mersa Matruh and even Benghazi, but he persuaded the parents to change their choice.

28 Tuesday

Dundee medical students chivalrously remove their red gowns and lay them in front of the Queen and the Duke of Edinburgh when heavy rain interrupts their visit. The students say they are inspired, 'by the foul weather and the memory of the first Elizabeth'.

. . . Eric Gates, footballer, born.. . .

29 Wednesday

The White House announces that between July 1957 and December 1958 the US will launch **unmanned satellites** into space that will circle the earth at a radius of 200-300 miles.

. . . THE DAILY TELEGRAPH celebrates its 100th birthday. . .

30 Thursday

A record number of cases of measles was recorded in June—27,000.

■ Britain invites Greece and Turkey to a conference on the future of **Cyprus.**
Final agreement is reached on the pay demands of the footplate men.

. . . The DOCK STRIKE is now in its sixth week. . .

THE STARS OF WIMBLEDON 1955

The first week of July is traditionally the time when the silverware is handed out at Wimbledon. And, for the first time since 1937, Britain could boast champions— doubles winners Angela Mortimer and Ann Shilcock (below). The singles crowns both headed across to the USA—Tony Trabert (left) and Louise Brough, storming to victory over Lennart Neilson and Beverley Baker Fleitz respectively.

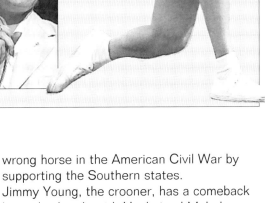

JULY
1 Friday
Dominion Day, Canada

Tony Trabert (USA) beats Lennart Neilsen (Den) 6-3, 7-5, 6-1, in the men's singles final at Wimbledon.
■ Four people are killed and two injured when a Meteor from RAF West Malling, Kent, crashes into strawberry pickers in a field adjoining the airstrip shortly after take-off.
■ Switzerland is suffering a glut of **asparagus.** 11,132,000lbs have been gathered so far in the Valais alone.

2 Saturday
The **Manchester Guardian** newspaper is 100 today. Calling itself 'an organ of British opinion', it admits to having backed the

wrong horse in the American Civil War by supporting the Southern states.
Jimmy Young, the crooner, has a comeback hit on his hands with Unchained Melody. Variety dates are flooding in, and the one-time electrician/baker/PT instructor/hair-dressing salon manager/rugby player celebrates with a full-page photograph in the NME and the caption 'I Returned'.
■ In the women's singles final at Wimbledon, Louise Brough (USA) beats Beverley Baker Fleitz (USA) 7-5, 8-6. **Angela Mortimer and Ann Shilcock** win the women's doubles. They are the first Britons to win a Wimbledon title since 1937.

3 Sunday
The Rev Kenneth Harper, (42), tee-total, non-smoking vicar of Brampton, Cumberland, suggests that the NHS should provide a pill, or an injection for those bridegrooms who

can't stand the strain. He remarks that after two or three weddings his church can smell like a brewery.

4 Monday
Independence Day, USA

Two Irish peers, Lord Nugent (37), 7th baron, 6ft , and Lord Kilbracken (35), 3rd baron, 6ft, are competing for a TV job with showgirl Vickie Bennet, a 23-year-old crooner, because Vickie's sponsors think her programme lacks tone. The job is worth £350 a week and means appearing in an American TV series. Lord Kilbracken has a university degree and was the Navy's youngest wartime Lieutenant-Commander, while Lord Nugent has made two films for British television.

■ **Colin Cowdrey,** the Kent cricketer who was discharged as medically unfit from the RAF in May, has been selected for England against South Africa in the Third Test starting at Old Trafford on Thursday .

5 Tuesday
Full Moon

The Minister of Transport, J Boyd-Carpenter, announces a new London-Yorkshire **motorway.** It is part of a plan to build a total of 345 miles of motor roads over the next 10 years, at an average costof £250,000 per mile.The first section to be built will be a 53-mile stretch at the London end.

■ A bang shakes south London at 12.15am and is heard as far away as Maidstone, Kent. It is caused by a Gloster Javelin aircraft breaking the sound barrier when the pilot inadvertently exceeds the speed of sound while freeing his oxygen tube from his parachute harness.

SPORT: Gordon Pirie runs 1 1/2 miles in 6mins 26secs and breaks the unofficial world record and English National record by 5.2 secs.

■ Barney Worth, who claimed to be the world's fattest man and at one time weighed 42 stone, dies in hospital in Bristol. When he became ill in his caravan at Severn Beach last week, it took six men to carry him to the ambulance. He and his wife used to travel the world as the fattest couple.

OFFICIAL: it's a scorcher! Temperatures of 78°F at Poole, Dorset and Leuchars, Fife, are recorded.

6 Wednesday

Psychologists at the Education Department in Kent have spent three years concluding that **unhappy children** do not like arithmetic because it doesn't offer an escape from unpleasant reality, and good readers have found 'a refuge from life'.

■ The convocations of Canterbury and York agree to their two Archbishops consulting on the possibility of closer relations with the Methodist Church .

■ Hottest day of the year— in Aberdeen reaches **80°F**— as Buenos Aires sees its first snow for 37 years.

7 Thursday

Sir Winston Churchill's new lion, Rota, sent as a present to him by the Lion Club International of Atlantic City, New Jersey, USA, arrives at London Zoo. He travelled by air, and is now in the quarantine section.

■ The Liverpool Philharmonic Society try out a **chocolate** that can be unwrapped without disturbing anyone.The box and wrapping are made of plastic material, and the audience love them.

. . . Hottest day of the year in London, with the temperature reaching 79°F. . .

8 Friday

Coal prices rise 17%, the biggest rise since nationalisation. Currently the standard summer retail price of Grade V coal is £4.15s. per ton. The new price will probably be £5.7s. per ton.

■ Methodist Conference authorizes a delegation to meet the Anglicans.

■ The French Government agrees to inde-

pendence for Tunisia. . .
GOLF: Peter Thomson, right, of Australia wins the Open at St Andrews. His score of 281 is a record for the Old Course.
■ Hottest day of the year so far, with a maximum temperature of 82.1°F and 14.2 hours of sunshine.

which was decided on the spur of the moment, says, 'I never saw kissin' like that in all my marryin' days.'
■ Thousands are caught in freak storms in London. Paving stones are thrown into the air by flood water, and lightning sends chimney stacks crashing all over the city. A landslide on the railway embankment at Wimbledon delays trains.

9 Saturday

Weathermen promise a warm, sunny weekend.
■ During its golden jubilee celebrations in Birmingham, the Austin Company unveils its experimental Austin Sheerline. It may look like any other car, but under the bonnet is a 125hp jet engine. Although there are still many problems to solve, experts think a jet car may be on sale in Britain in 1957.

10 Sunday

A hot and dusty family arrive at Woburn Abbey, with steam hissing from the engine of their 21year-old car. The owner, Claude Tramson, asks for water for the radiator, and he gets a magnum of champagne, too. Claude's wife, Gladys, is the 100,000th visitor to the Abbey since it opened. The Duke also presents Mrs Tramson with a framed print of the Abbey and a copy of a book *Life in a Noble House*.
. . . The amnesty offered to May Mau rebels ends, after 1,000 have surrendered. . .
■ The Soho Fair in London opens. The organisers hope that it will help to rid Soho of its seedy underworld image.

11 Monday

Clark Gable (54), marries wife number five, **Kay Williams Spreckell** (37), at Minden, Nevada. Walter Fischer, the Justice of the Peace who conducted the runaway wedding,

12 Tuesday

Ascot races finally take place, having been postponed in June because of the rail strike.
CRICKET: South Africa win the Third Test.
■ Hottest day of the year: in Kendal, Westmoreland, the temperature reaches 87°F and at Manchester airport it is 83°F.

13 Wednesday

Despite a demonstration of nearly 400 people outside Holloway Prison, and much public feeling against it, **Ruth Ellis** is **hanged** at 9am for the murder of her lover, racing driver David Blakely, outside a pub in Hampstead on Easter Sunday. Thousands of people gather in Hyde Park to hear speeches against capital punishment.
■ The Isle of Capri witnesses the meeting of two of the biggest names in show business when the Onassis yacht, *Christina*, docks, and **Greta Garbo** comes ashore. She meets **Gracie Fields** at the Canzone del Mare swimming pool. Miss Garbo makes one of her famous 'I want to be alone' speeches to the gathered reporters and photographers.
■ MPs queue to meet **Marlene Dietrich** who is visiting the House of Commons as a guest of **Mrs Bessie Braddock**. (See picture, facing page). After lunch in the Strangers' dining-room she sits in the gallery through Question Time and takes tea on the terrace.

14 Thursday

Lightning strikes the crowd at Royal Ascot this afternoon, killing one women and injuring 46 other racegoers.

BESSIE and MARLENE: Commons date

of Britain. It is the most strenuous amateur cycle race in Europe and the contestants have to cycle 1,000 miles in nine days.
■ Billy Knight and Roger Becker, Britain's young **Davis Cup** team, lose the first two singles to the experienced Italian team of Nicolo Pietrangeli and Fausto Gardini.

16 Saturday

A seven-mile queue of **traffic** is recorded on the Blackpool-Preston road and a temperature of 90°F is recorded at the Harrow meteorological office.
■ Catholic primate, **Cardinal Mindszenty**, is released from jail in Hungary and is placed under house arrest.
■ It is the hottest day in London for two years, with temperatures reaching 84°F. 50,000 vehicles an hour are leaving the city.

17 Sunday

SUMMIT LINE-UP (from left): Bulganin, Eisenhower, Faure and Eden

SUMMIT: The Big Three Western leaders - the US **President Eisenhower**, British Prime Minister **Sir Anthony Eden** and French Prime Minister **Edgar Faure**— meet in Geneva in preparation for the summit conference with **Mr Khruschev** and **President Bulganin** tomorrow.
■ Stirling Moss, driving a Mercedes Benz, wins his first Grand Prix, beating world champion racing driver and team mate, Juan Fangio (Brazil) in the British Grand Prix.
■ An earthquake in Turkey kills four and injures 25. Nearly 600 houses are destroyed and 1,000 damaged.

■ A cold lunch for 5s. 6d. will be served on holiday **expresses** to and from Euston and St Pancras on Saturdays. Cold meat, salad and potatoes will be followed by fruit, or cheese and biscuits. London Midland Railways hope this will enable them to serve more meals in less time.

15 Friday
ST SWITHIN'S DAY

Seventy-five cyclists in teams of five leave Whitworth Park, Manchester on the first lap of the amateur circuit

18 Monday

President Eisenhower toasts Soviet **President Bulganin** (left) at a men-only banquet in Geneva during the **Big Four** peace talks, which have been chiefly noted for friendly speeches. It is the first time for 10 years that the leaders of the USA and the USSR have met face-to-face.

■ **Disneyland** opens at Anaheim, California. Walt Disney's 160 acres of fantasy and fun cost $17 million to build.

■ Following the death of **Ruth Ellis**, a poll in the Daily Mirror comes out two-to-one against hanging. 37% of women are in favour of retaining the death penalty, against 32% of men.

■ American Negro singer **Paul Robeson** is once again refused a US passport. He was originally denied a passport in 1950 for refusing to sign an affidavit stating whether he was or ever had been a member of the Communist party. He has a concert tour booked in England, as well as the offer of the part of Othello in London.

19 Tuesday
New Moon

Four men steal a van delivering money to the British Linen Bank in Paisley Road West, Glasgow, and get away with between £30,000-£40,000.

■ Figures released today reveal that 6,000 fewer national servicemen were called up in 1954 than in 1953.

20 Wednesday

Calouste Gulbenkian (96), **Mr 5%**, dies alone in an hotel in Lisbon. He got his nickname after the 1914-1918 war when he sold his concession on all oil produced in Iraq to the Iraq Petroleum Company for 5% of the profits in perpetuity. His fortune is estimated at more than £300 million.

■ The Lord Mayor's National Flood and Tempest Distress Fund reached £6,550,000 during the first three months of this year.

■ The **Kremlin** opens its doors to the public for the first time since 1923. . .

21 Thursday

Britain's dollar income from American and Canadian **tourists** last year was enough to pay for all the tobacco and wheat we imported from the USA. The number of US tourists was up 9% on the previous year, to 203,000.

■ A **radar scanner** has been installed on the roof of Victory House (the Met Office) to see if it will forecast the approach of heavy rain. If it works, other big cities will get one.

■ Gordonstoun School, Moray, Scotland, one of whose most illustrious pupils was the Duke of Edinburgh, is forming its own mountain rescue unit.

22 Friday

The British **Admiralty** is showing interest in two new broadcasting systems, UHF and VHF, developed by the Massachusetts Institute of Technology, Boston, USA .

23 Saturday

Donald Campbell (above), sets a new world water-speed record of 202.53mph on Lake Ullswater in the Lake District.

■ Frederick Oldman (39) of Huddersfield, sets a new record of 4hrs 53mins for swimming the 10 1/2 mile length of Lake Windermere.

■ **Cordell Hull** (84), American statesman,

Secretary of State from 1933 to 1944 and winner of the Nobel Peace prize, in 1945, has died.

24 Sunday

Customs and Excise are asked to release seven gold watches, brought back by a party of British journalist who were given them by **King Saud** of Saudi Arabia. Customs assess the duty at £8 6s. 8d. and value the watches at £10 each. The journalists decline to pay the duty.
■ **Pat Smythe** on Prince Hal wins the Daily Mail Cup at the **International Horse Show** at White City.

25 Monday

Singapore votes 28-1 in favour of self-government.
CRICKET: England, set to make 481 in the Fourth Test against South Africa, need 366 in six hours with eight wickets in hand.
. . . DR CARL JUNG, psychiatrist, is 80 today. . .
■ A new **helicopter** service between the south bank of the Thames at Battersea and Heathrow Airport starts today.

26 Tuesday

The **Chancellor** of the Exchequer, **R A Butler** (right) says there is no economic crisis and the £ will not be devalued from its current level of £1 = $2.80.
■ Delays at the docks have grown worse since the strike. Sometimes lorries are waiting several days to be unloaded.
■ England lose the Fourth Test to South Africa, by 224 runs.

27 Wednesday

At the end of a statement to the House of Commons on the **Big Four** meeting in Geneva last week, Sir Anthony Eden

announces that the Soviet Premier **Marshal Bulganin** and Communist Party Secretary Nikita Khruschev will visit Britain next year.
BORN: Allan Border, Australian cricketer.

28 Thursday

The **BBC** say that from September 4, it will increase its television output by about 15 hours a week. The BBC's annual report also reveals that it allocated only £5,043,908 to television last year against £10,018,77 for radio, despite the average nightly audience for television being bigger than that for the Home, Light and Third programmes combined.

29 Friday

Cambridge University is given £100,000 in ten instalments by Mullard, Ltd. to set up an astronomical observatory.
■ The BBC **Light Programme** celebrates its 10th birthday.

30 Saturday

Whitsun holiday. 31,000 cars an hour are leaving London.
■ A **glider pilot** taking part in a National Gliding Championship event from Lasham Airfield, Hants, makes a forced landing in a field and is charged repeatedly by a bull. The bull holes the glider in three places. Luckily, when the rescuers arrive, the bull turns his attention to their car.
■ **Christopher Chataway** (above) sets a new world record for three miles of 13mins 22.2secs in the match against Germany at White City .
. . . Chinese premier Chou En-Lai calls for an Asian-Pacific Peace Pact. . .

31 Sunday

Joseph Sykes, of Morley, Lancs, drives the 12 miles from Filey to Bridlington trying to get rid of the swarm of **bees** on the front

axle and number plate of his car. They hang like great bunches of grapes.
■ **Marilyn Bell** (17—pictured at Dover prior to her brave crossing) of Toronto, Canada, becomes the youngest girl to swim the **Channel,** in 14hrs 30mins
■ **July** has been the sunniest and driest for 86 years.

AUGUST

1 Monday

BANK HOLIDAY

The sunniest Bank Holiday Monday for many years. Motorists arriving at Porthcothan Bay, N Cornwall, find it surrounded by a moat. **Holidaymakers** have dug a trench across its width and filled it with water to stop cars driving on the sand.
■ J Russell of Downham Market, Norfolk, driving a Cooper, wins the *Daily Telegraph* International Challenge Trophy for Formula III cars at Brands Hatch, with an average speed of 71.16mph.

2 Tuesday

More than 1,000 cases of **polio** have been reported in England and Wales so far this year .
■ The major portion of a **human skull** estimated to be between 100,000-250,000 years old is discovered in the gravel pits at Swanscombe, Kent.

3 Wednesday
Full Moon

The Ministry of Housing and Local Government urges local authorities to create green belts to prevent the unrestricted **sprawl** of great cities.
■ A **Canberra** twin-jet photo-reconnaissance plane flies London-New York-London in 14hrs 21mins 45.4secs, setting the record for the double journey.

■ No-passport jaunts to **Boulogne** are proving so popular that many restaurants at the Channel port are serving ham, eggs, fish and steak, all with chips 'and a nice cup of tea'.
... EAMONN ANDREWS is to compere a TV series called 'This is Your Life' starting this autumn ...

4 Thursday

Queen Elizabeth **the Queen Mothe**r celebrates her 55th birthday at Clarence House. Prince Charles and Princess Anne are her first callers.
■ Large parts of the USA are suffering the worst **drought** for 40 years.

5 Friday

Waiting for Godot, by Samuel Becket, produced by Peter Hall and starring Paul Daneman and Peter Woodthorpe, opens in London at the Little Arts Theatre Club to a hostile reception from the critics. Samuel Becket was at one time James Joyce's secretary.
■ Film star **Carmen Miranda** (40), left, renowned for her dancing and exotic hats, dies. She made her film debut in *Down Argentina Way*.

6 Saturday

It's the 10th anniversary of the dropping of the **atomic bomb** on Hiroshima.
■ 80,000 Russian soccer fans see Moscow Spartak beat Britain's **Wolves** (right) led by the England captain, **Billy Wright**, 3-0 in the Moscow

Dynamo stadium. Hundreds of thousands more Russian fans watch the game on TV or hear it on the radio.

7 Sunday

The 10.35am Manchester to London **express** fouls the points near Rugby and plunges down a 12ft embankment. The driver, is killed, and the fireman is badly scalded, but only 19 of the 250 passengers are injured, one of them seriously.
■ Mohammed Ali **resigns** as prime minister of Pakistan.

8 Monday

The Queen opens the National Library of Wales at Aberystwyth, while Prince Charles and Princess Anne go bathing at deserted Whattick Bay.
■ International runner **Chris Chataway** is to become a newscaster on commercial television. He recently broke the world 3-mile record in a time of 13mins 23.2secs, and hopes to run in next year's Olympic Games in Melbourne, Australia.

9 Tuesday

300 miners are trapped by fire for two hours in a pit shaft at Grassmoor Colliery, nr Chesterfield, but all of them are brought out safely.
■ The US airforce base at Burtonwood, nr. Warrington, is appointing secret traffic spotters to watch out for traffic violations by its own **US airmen**, but also to note acts of courteous driving.

10 Wednesday

Scientists at the Radiofarm Institute in Rome are using **atomic energy** to ripen wheat in 64 days—five months less than normal. The wheat also shows a 45% increase in the number of grains on the ears.
■ The **Duke of Veruga**, a direct descendant of Christopher Columbus, is first home in the 605-mile Fastnet Race in the Spanish yacht *Mare Nostrum*. It left Cowes on Saturday and reaches Plymouth today.

■ A **NAAFI** (Navy Army and Air Force Institutes) survey shows that the navy is drinking more milk than beer, and the Army and RAF more tea, coffee and soft drinks. The favourite meal is egg and chips.

11 Thursday

London is to get a new evening paper, **The Sun**. It will have a special racing service and be politically independent.
■ The nine-year-old British Friesian **cow** Weeton Cutie 11th, which has won all the highest awards open to a British dairy cow, sweeps the board at the Royal Lancashire Show, and wins the gold medal as champion cow.

12 Friday

The extra-mural department of Manchester University is offering a Latin refresher course for adults who want to help their children with their homework.
■ The 200,000 workers in the wholesale tailoring, mantle and costume industry, three-

quarters of whom are women, will receive the following **pay rises**: men an extra 2d. an hour (about 7s.4d. a week); women an extra 1 1/2d. an hour (about 5s. a week) and juveniles between 1d. and 1 1/2d. an hour.

■ Road signs in London are to carry the words, 'Courtesy, everybody, please', for three months.

■ Thomas Mann (80), the great German novelist and **Nobel prizewinner**, author of *Death in Venice* and *The Magic Mountain*, dies in Zurich.

13 Saturday

A plot to attack army garrisons, radio stations, police stations, power stations, water works and communications, and kill **President Peron** (right), is uncovered in Buenos Aires. Police make arrests.

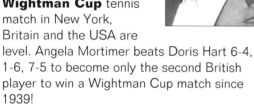

■ After the first day of the **Wightman Cup** tennis match in New York, Britain and the USA are level. Angela Mortimer beats Doris Hart 6-4, 1-6, 7-5 to become only the second British player to win a Wightman Cup match since 1939!

14 Sunday

Abdel Latif Abu Heif (27) from Egypt, wins the Butlin's Cross Channel race in 11hrs 44mins from Thomas Laurie Park (31) of California, 16 mins behind. Neither of them beat the record of 10hrs 50mins set by another Egyptian, Abdel Rehim in 1950. Damain Boltran of Mexico was third. Only three of the 16 starters finished.

■ The Board of Trade say that, after 15 years, government controls over the size of **newspapers** will end in March 1956.

■ The Royal Academy's Summer Exhibition has broken all attendance records since World War 1. Over 250,000 have visited thanks to one portrait—the **Queen** by Italy's Pietro Annigoni.

Born: Ed Moses, US athlete

HAPPY AN

GLORIOUS—THE WINDSORS

HOWZAT! ENGLAND WIN SERIES AGAINST SOUTH AFRICA

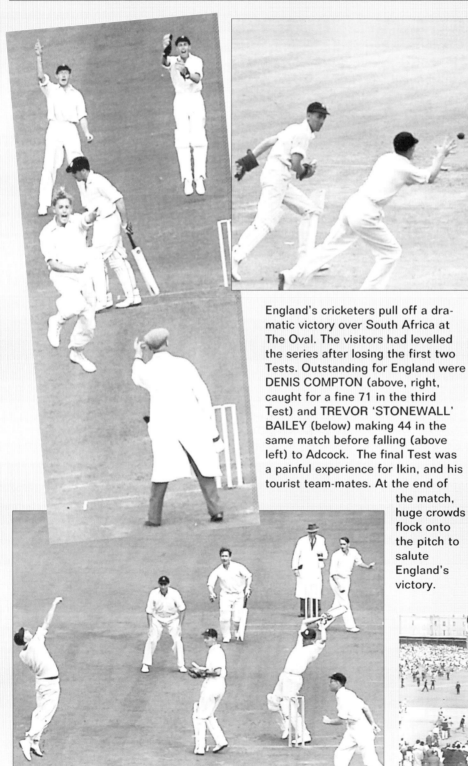

England's cricketers pull off a dramatic victory over South Africa at The Oval. The visitors had levelled the series after losing the first two Tests. Outstanding for England were DENIS COMPTON (above, right, caught for a fine 71 in the third Test) and TREVOR 'STONEWALL' BAILEY (below) making 44 in the same match before falling (above left) to Adcock. The final Test was a painful experience for Ikin, and his tourist team-mates. At the end of the match, huge crowds flock onto the pitch to salute England's victory.

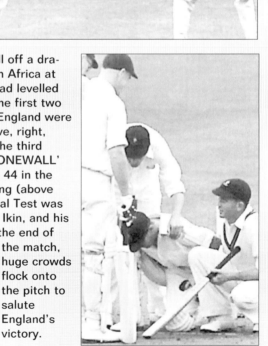

15 Monday

Princess Anne (right) is five today. She celebrates her birthday at Balmoral.

■ Alan Crompton (28), captain of the British Olympic skiing team, crosses the **Channel** from Dover to Calais and back in three hours. He is towed at cable's length behind a speedboat piloted by Donald Campbell, holder of the world water-speed record.

TENNIS: The USA score their 19th successive win over Britain in the Wightman Cup played in New York, 6-1.

16 Tuesday

The **New York Times** newspaper and **Time** magazine attack Britain's popular daily newspapers, calling them the least informative in the world. Apart from the three quality papers—*The Times*, the *Manchester Guardian* and the *Daily Telegraph*—the other six daily papers, with a combined circulation of 14 million, extend by degrees to the 'wildest and most sensational in the world'.

17 Wednesday

New Moon

Poachers are stealing **water** from the 'filling stations' for local farmers whose ponds have dried up in the villages of Flagg and Monyash, nr Bakewell, Derbyshire.The drain on the reservoir serving the villages is such that the local people frequently find their taps have run dry.

■ The president of the West German Automobile Club thinks that **British drivers** are the politest in the world, and British roads make for good driving.

■ Nationalist agitators in Casablanca, **Morocco,** smash street lights and daub the walls with slogans calling for holy war against French rule.

CRICKET: England win the Fifth Test and the series against South Africa, 3-2.

■ **Fernand Léger** (74), a member of the cubist movement and known for the largeness of scale and strong colour of his paintings, dies.

18 Thursday

A Coventry motor engineer, Leonard Warren (38), accused of **stealing** £23,800, said that when the escort put the notes in his car to take to the bank's head office he 'just drove off with it'. He said he had committed the offence because he was being blackmailed by a woman he couldn't name as 'she was too high in society'.

19 Friday

It is revealed that **Clement Attlee** (72), leader of the Labour party, suffered a cerebral thrombosis shortly after his return

JANE . . .

from holiday in Yugoslavia about ten days ago. Mrs Attlee says he has completely recovered from the attack.

■ Angry passengers from the liner **Orontes**, docked at Southampton, try to force their way back on board to retrieve their baggage, which is being held because of a **dispute** with stevedores.

20 Saturday
Moslem New Year AH 1375

The **Chicago Tribune** announces that it will abandon most of its 'simplified spelling'. For 20 years the paper has used spellings of its own, 'frate' for 'freight', 'photograf' for 'photograph', for example, in the hope that it would make learning to read easier. Teachers now say that it makes learning to read harder. The paper will continue to use 'tho', thru and thoro'.

21 Sunday

Group Captain **Peter Townsend**, on holiday with his sons in Ostend, deals affably with the 50 reporters who have been following him all weekend. **Princess Margaret** is 25 today, and could, if she wished, tell parliament of her desire to marry without seeking the Queen's permission. A birthday prayer is said for the princess during the service at Crathie Church, Balmoral, where she is celebrating her birthday. 10,000 sightseers greet her outside the church.

■ It's 91°F in Jersey, and a warm, sunny day in the south turns the roads into 'a second bank holiday'. The autumn illuminations are turned on at Southend, Essex.

22 Monday

The Commonwealth **Trans-Antarctic expedition** have decided to name the base they will establish at Vahsel Bay on the Weddell Sea the Shackleton Base, after Sir Ernest Shackleton.

■ More than 1,600 men, women

and children, French and Arab, died during a weekend of **rioting** in French North Africa. Yesterday the French Army opened what it called a 'very violent' clean-up campaign against the Arab rebels. The French open peace talks.

23 Tuesday

Parts of northern England have their **hottest** day for years with temperatures in the 80's. Liverpool has its warmest day since 1948, reaching 83.2°F. Weston-Super-Mare records a high of 89°F.

■ An English Electric Canberra Jet **bomber** becomes the first aircraft to fly London-New/NewYork-London in a day. The average speed of East-West journey is 461.12mph, and the West-East journey is 550.12mph. The average speed overall is 481.52mph. The 7,000 mile round trip took under 15 hours, and the flight back from New York was 13mins less than the fastest train journey from King's Cross to Edinburgh.

24 Wednesday

The residents of St Etienne, France, call the police to trap an **escaped** 'tiger cub', but when the police arrive they find it is a big yellow cat. However, its owner turns out to be an escaped convict. so their journey isn't wasted.

. . . BEA announce their first profitable year. . .

25 Thursday

It is suggested that Scottish **maths teaching** should include a study of income tax and local rates, with pupils given actual forms to work with. It is also recommended that boys

Three of the four new stamps on sale from September

should learn how to use steel rules and joiners' foot rules, while girls should be taught to use an inch tape as well as a ruler.
■ Actor **Sean Connery** celebrates his 25th birthday.

26 Friday

Vegetable-growers in South Devon are under attack by thousands of **caterpillars**; at Totnes, they have already killed a field of kale, and in many places only bare stalks remain of once flourishing fields.
■ The Leeds **Budgerigar** Society meeting at Leeds Town Hall attracts a record 1,400 entries from all over the country.
■ A **thunderstorm** with torrential rain stops the harvest in Suffolk and puts all the telephones in Woodbridge out of action. 24,000 people in the Rhymney Valley, South Wales are forbidden to draw any water for 15 hours each night.
... SURREY are County Cricket champions for the fourth successive year...

27 Saturday

A 48-year-old widow with five children and one grandchild, who has lived in a hut on Castle Donington Airfield, Leics, for 10yrs, is fined £2 for not having a **radio licence**. When the Bench discovers that Mrs Webster cares for her family on just £7 a week, they approach the Queen for Royal forgiveness of the fine, and it is remitted.

28 Sunday

W Pickering, of Bloxwich, Staffs, sets a new record for **swimming** the Channel in 14hrs 6mins. The previous record of 14hrs 42 mins

was set by Florence Chadwick of California, in 1953.
■ The National Youth **Orchestra,** conducted by Sir Adrian Boult, perform for the first time at a Promenade Concert at the Royal Albert Hall, London.

29 Monday

The Royal Australian Navy wants to recruit 1,000 men in Great Britain. Former Naval ratings are preferred, and men may bring their wives and families.
■ A conference of the British, Greek and Turkish governments on the eastern Mediterranean and **Cyprus** begins in London.
■ Egyptian and Israeli fighters clash over Gaza for the first time since 1948.
■ Film star **Rita Hayworth** (36), above, announces her separation from her fourth husband, crooner Dick Haymes.

30 Tuesday

Dundee Town Council recommend the building of a **road bridge** over the river Tay.
■ Whisky goes up 1s. a bottle to 36s.
■ A new 2 1/2-litre BRM driven by Peter Collins will have its first race on Saturday.

31 Wednesday

The president of the National Union of Railwaymen says that French trains are cleaner, faster and more comfortable, probably because of **electrification.** France has already electrified 3,000 miles of track, with a further 700 miles in the process, and has spent £220 million on the railway system since the war. Britain could achieve the same if the will to spend the money was there.

THE WORLD'S TROUBLE S

MAU MAU atrocities continue unabated throughout 1955 even though the Governor, Sir Evelyn Baring, offers an amnesty to the terrorists in January. They are told they will not hang, though they may be held in detention.

The amnesty terms are withdrawn in July, when 1,000 terrorists have surrendered. In the past three years of Mau Mau activity, 13,000 people have died and 70,000 people have been jailed.

Continuing trouble in **CYPRUS.** The EOKA terrorist organisation, led by George Grivas, continues its bombing campaign to overthrow the government. British troops are helping the police,

RAF planes are patrolling the shores, and a Royal Navy frigate is anchored in Morphou Bay.

A British government invitation to tripartite talks is welcomed by the island's Turkish community, but the Greek leaders under Archbishop Makarios, insist that formal recognition by the British of the principal of self-determination is a prerequisite for any conference.

Talks open in September, but almost immediately break up. EOKA is outlawed by the British, and there are violent demonstrations against British rule, followed by a General Strike. The Governor, Sir John Harding, declares a state of emergency.

The French continue to fight nationlist uprisings in North Africa. Martial law is imposed in **MOROCCO.**

Civil War breaks out between North and South **VIETNAM.**

The Army patrols the streets of Lefkoniko, scene tion raid on a police station by EOKA terrorists,

MAU MAU (right) continue to commit atrocities despite an amnesty offer. In MOROCCO (inset, above), there are protests against French rule.

TS OF 1955

t arms and ammuni-
ge Grivas (below)

£10,000 REWARD

£10,000 will be paid to any member of the public who gives information leading to the arrest of

GEORGE THEODORUS GRIVAS

whose photographs and description are given below

DESCRIPTION.—Age about 56. height 5 feet 6 inches medium to broad build (possibly less thick set than indicated in photograph) strong broad face, small Hitler-style moustache, chestnut hair, bald on top (hair greying above ears and on temples), chestnut eyes, dark and bushy eyebrows, EARS ARE LARGE AND SET LOW ON HEAD, wide shut mouth with firm jaw.

ANYONE who gives this information will be given

£10,000 IN CASH

(or the equivalent in other sterling currency) and, if he or she desires, be taken into protective custody, and will be given a free passage by sea or air with British protection to any place in the world he or she desires outside CYPRUS. The journey will be kept secret and so arranged that the destination will not become known.

BY ORDER OF THE GOVERNMENT OF CYPRUS
3rd May, 1956

SEPTEMBER

1 Thursday

The PO issue four **new stamps** depicting the Queen with four castles—£1 Windsor; 10s. Edinburgh; 5s. Caernarvon; 2s. 6d. Carrickfergus.

■ Burton-upon-Trent, Staffs, council members all have their heads measured as they are to be issued with **official hats**.

■ It is now an offence to have an electric motor that causes interference with radio and television reception. If you have a vacuum cleaner, drill or hair dryer that upsets your neighbour's listening or viewing, you will have to fit a suppressor.

. . . Partridge shooting begins. . .

2 Friday
Full Moon

Laughter at Work

"It's probably the foreman — I couldn't bear him either."

At the British Association for the Advancement of Science meeting in Bristol, **brain** expert Dr Grey Walter shows off Topsy (toposcope) and Annie (analysis of brain waves), machines that can help you pick the right husband or wife. The patient sits under a whalebone and rubber cover, like a hairdryer, and the machine records brain activity to show how well people get on with one another.

■ Britain's **gold** and dollar reserves (£819 million) are at their lowest point for more than two years, and less than they were at the end of World War II.

3 Saturday

Space experts say that the runaway research balloon carrying 15 mice and guinea pigs, which was launched from Minnesota on Thursday to test the effects of space rays on live animals, is now so far

THE SHAPE OF CARS IN 1955

A chrome-lover's delight! This year's models (clockwise), the Armstrong Siddeley Sapphire, Austin Sheerline, Citroen, and Jaguar 2.4.

4

above the stratosphere that it has become a satellite.

■ Details are announced today of the new Bentley Continental **sports saloon**, the most expensive standard car in production in Britain. It costs just £7,027 15s. 10d (purchase tax £2,067 16s. 10d.— enough to buy four small family cars), has a top speed of 120mph and does 18 miles per gallon.

■ Israel accepts UN **ceasefire** in Gaza.

Sunday

The BBC's plans to put out a further 15 hours of programmes a week in the run-up to the start of **commercial television** on September 22 have been stopped by the Postmaster General, who feels it would be unfair to the rival television companies to start the extra transmissions as planned.

5 Monday

Delegates to the TUC general conference recommend that the **school leaving age** should be raised to 16, no later than 1960.

■ The Dutch Grand Prix is won by Juan **Fangio** (Brazil) driving a Mercedes Benz with Stirling Moss, also driving a Mercedes Benz, second. Just one length divided them.

■ Opening of the **Farnborough Air Show**. It is announced at the National Aircraft Show in Philadelphia, USA, that a US F100C Supersabre set a new level-flight speed record of 822.1mph over an 11 mile course at the Edwards Airforce base, California, on August 20.

6 Tuesday

Commercial television presents a sample hour of the new televison programmes coming to the south of England on September 22. The demonstration takes place in a London restaurant. It begins with a tea-planter talking about tea blending. This is followed by 30mins of **Robin Hood** starring **Richard Greene**, 1min of advertisements and **I Love Lucy**. The verdict is that the advertisements are a bit childish, but I Love Lucy is well ahead of anything that can be seen on BBC.

■ Group Captain **Peter Townsend**, visiting Britain for the Farnborough Air Show, pays a visit to the Queen Mother's private secretary in St James's Palace.

. . .A force of British commandos is sent to Cyprus amid mounting tension. . .

Wednesday

Nearly 1,000 shop assistants at Bourne & Hollingsworth department store, London, will get four week's **holiday** a year, plus Easter, Christmas and Bank Holidays, if they agree to work until 8pm each Thursday. The shop assistants love the idea. Their union says, 'We'll call a meeting to discuss it.'

■ A **psychologist** at London's Tavistock Clinic, reporting on his blush study, says that blushers get upset more when they are watched at work and try and hide it by getting sun-lamp tans and faking coughing fits.

Thursday

Gardener William McLoughlin (29) so **terrified** Ms Bertha Smith (75), that she gave him £10,000 over a five-year period. He sent her many letters demanding money, telling her that his wife had died, and his daughter had been killed. She finally sought help when he presented her with a letter, supposedly from a doctor, saying he had only six months to live, and she should give him whatever he wanted.

■ British authorities in Berlin are asking for the return of two British **soldiers** who fell asleep in a train and were taken into the Soviet zone.

■ There are rave reviews for **Kenneth Williams**, who plays the boy editor in the

new musical The Buccaneer by Sandy Wilson, author of *The Boyfriend*.

■ Lady Zia Wernher's **Meld** (W H Carr), follows her victory in the Oaks by winning the St Leger by 3/4 length from Nucleus (L Piggott).

Friday

The Soviet ambassador to Britain, **Jacob Malik,** switches on the Blackpool illuminations—a banner bearing the words 'Peace and Goodwill' surrounded by lights—and is presented with a 3ft stick of rock with his name running through it.

■ The TUC Congress calls on the government to cut the call-up as too many young men are wasting their time in the forces, while productive industries are short of young employees.

Saturday

The queue for the last bus at Shenfield, Essex, is startled by an explosion inside the Westminster Bank. Detectives rush into the bank, and the **thief** jumps through a plate-glass window, landing among the bus queue.

SEPTEMBER

■ 600 British commandos arrive in **Cyprus** in the campaign against Greek terrorists fighting for Enosis (union with Greece).

11 Sunday

A further 900 British commando reinforcements arrive in Cyprus.
■ Reginald Swabey (75), leads 50 people past the notice saying 'Admission 1s. 6d.' at Willesden's Annual Show in Roundwood Park, waving a letter from the Ministry of Housing and Local Government and telling the crowds the charge is illegal. An LCC official says Willesden Council could have charged had they previously officially closed the park.
■ 400 French call-up men, mainly Air Force ground crew, **mutiny** at the Gare de Lyon, Paris, saying they do not want to go to Morocco.

12 Monday

Britain is to hold a third series of A-Bomb tests in the Monte Bello Islands, of the NW coast of Australia next April.
■ Farmer Ken Cutcliffe (49) of Swanswick, Hants, is attacked and knocked down three times by his bull. His son Michael (9), grabs a pitchfork and charges the bull, allowing his father to get away.
■ 16 people are killed and 120 injured when an **earthquake** shakes Cairo, Egypt. It is the worst earthquake there for 30 years.

13 Tuesday

London Zoo proudly shows off its new baby —a 3-day-old hog deer. It weighed just 1lb at birth and stands just 10ins high. HMS Vanguard, the Royal Navy's only

active-service battleship and its biggest at 44,500 tons, is retired from service.
■ Don Cockell, the British and Empire Heavyweight champion retires after three rounds against the Cuban Nino Valdes at White City.

14 Wednesday

New Moon

Gordon Pirie beats the Czech wonderman **Emil Zatopek (picture, left)** by a yard to win the 5,000 metres in Prague.
■ Blue **jeans** for women have become the number one best selling garment this summer, in the wake of their sisters in the USA and Canada.

15 Thursday

Britain's athletes win a great victory over Czechoslovakia in Prague, the men's team winning by 117-98 points and the women's team by 58-48 points. Zatopek gains his revenge on Pirie.

16 Friday

The entire **night shift** at St Mary's Railway Goods Wharf, Derby, is accused of **stealing** or receiving goods. Cameras, stockings, underwear and dresses have gone missing.The men used a homemade hook to extract goods from wicker hampers without tampering with the lock.

17 Saturday
Jewish New Year AM 5716

More trouble in **Cyprus.** Gangs of Cypriots set fire to the British Institute in Nicosia.
■ The **Queen** has ordered all the royal TV sets to be adapted to receive commercial

70

FAIRYTALE WEDDING OF THE YEAR

A gondola ride from the church is the focus for the world's cameramen, gathered for the wedding of the year. The canals of Venice provide the perfect backdrop for the wedding of **Princess Ira von Fuerstenberg** and **Prince Alfonso Hohenlohe-Langenberg**.

television transmissions before the Royal Family return from Balmoral.

18 Sunday

1,000 Cypriot youths run wild in **Nicosia.** The British Institute is now a smoking ruin.
■ 15th anniversary of the **Battle of Britain** is commemorated. 12 stained-glass windows are unveiled at the RAF station, Biggin Hill, designed by Hugh Easton who made the Battle of Britain memorial window in Westminster Abbey.
■ In Russia, **Vladimir Kuts** sets a new world record for the 5,000 metres of 14 minutes, 46.8 seconds.
. . . Bob Dylan celebrates his 22nd birthday, and Greta Garbo, her 50th. . .

19 Monday

The Foreign Office admits that parts of the report of Vladimir Petrov, the former Soviet diplomat in Australia, confirm that **Burgess** and **Maclean** were long-term Soviet agents, and that they had been suspected of

being **spies** for many years before they fled the country in May 1951.

20 Tuesday

Juan Peron (60), dictator of Argentina for nine years, **flees** the country in a Paraguayan gun boat which takes him to Asuncion, Paraguay, where he has been granted asylum.
■ New **cars** are appearing in brighter colours, but you have to pay extra for the 'New Gay Look'. You can buy a two-tone pastel-coloured Hillman Minx for £687, an increase of £37.
■ British athlete **Diane Leather** smashes her own world record for the mile by 5secs, in a time of 4mins 15secs.

21 Wednesday

The **wedding of the year** between Prince Alfonso Hohenlohe-Langenberg (39) and Princess Ira von Fuerstenberg (15) takes place in Venice. The decor for the wedding breakfast is black, scarlet and gold, like the

ON THE AIR—INDEPENDENT TV

Billy Cotton gets commercial television off and kicking—while the first commercial is for Gibbs SR toothpaste.

gondola procession, and has been designed by Oliver Messel; the pageboys wear white lace, black velvet breeches and dark green sashes, and the church is packed with gardenias, carnations, and 250 photographers.
■ The Government announce that the Royal Navy has undertaken the formal annexation of the uninhabited island of **Rockall,** as it may come within the orbit of any projected weapons range in the Hebrides.

22 Thursday

Independent television goes on the air in London with *The Billy Cotton Band Show* from Wood Green Empire, and the news, read by Christopher Chataway. The first advertisement is for **Gibbs SR** toothpaste.
■ In an effort to retain listeners, **BBC Radio** counter-attacks with Grace Archer being killed dashing into a blazing stable to rescue a horse in *The Archers*.
. . . HURRICANES in the West Indies. Many killed. . .

23 Friday

The Government White Paper on **spies** Guy Burgess and Donald Maclean admits they were watched for two years, but only in London. They were not followed into the country, 'in case they smelled a rat'. Foreign Secretary **Harold Macmillan** takes the blame when the pace and manner of the investigation is questioned.

24 Saturday

US **President Eisenhower** suffers a slight heart-attack, and is in hospital in Denver. Political observers are now sure that he will not seek a second term in office.
■ The World Accordian Championship at Brighton is won by Kurt Heusser (20), of St Gallen, Switzerland.

25 Sunday

Donald Campbell flies to the USA. He is paying a preliminary visit to Lake Mead, Nevada, where he hopes to beat the 202mph record he set on Lake Ullswater in July. Bluebird follows by air freight.

■ A **model aeroplane** owned by Ray Gibbs (21) of Ilford, Essex, and fuelled by castor oil, breaks the world speed record at the All-Britain Model Aircraft Rally at Radlett, Herts, with a speed of 146mph.

26 Monday

First half of the £15 million **transatlantic telephone** cable, the first across the Atlantic seabed, is laid by the Post Office Telegraph ship Monarch. For the first time Newfoundland and Britain are linked by submarine cable. The second cable, completing the system and carrying speech the other way, will be laid in 1956.

■ **Admiral Raeder** (79), wartime Commander in Chief of the German Navy, is released from Spandau because of ill-health.

■ Michael Caborn Waterfield (25), amateur steeplechase rider and ex-fiance of film star **Diana Dors** appears at Bow Street Magistrate's Court charged with jumping on the back of her husband, Denis Gittins (30) outside London's Embassy Club. There seemed to be no reason for the attack, and Mr Caborn Waterfield is fined 20s.

■ Bird's Eye **fish fingers** go on sale in Britain.

. . . HUGHIE GREENE's show, 'Double Your Money', starts on ITV. . .

■ President Eisenhower, recovering from his slight heart-attack, is satisfactory.

27 Tuesday

The voice of **TIM,** the speaking clock, is precisely 20 years old. TIM has answered more than 515 million calls. The voice has never become hoarse because it is hermetically sealed on four glass discs. The voice was chosen from more than 15,000 telephonists who entered a competition.

■ **Dr Roger Bannister** is to conduct interviews and commentate on athletics exclusively for the BBC.

■ NBC in New York have entered into discussions with the BBC about buying *The Goon Show*.

28 Wednesday

Jaguar launch a cheaper car. Shorter, narrower and lighter than the Mark VII saloon it has a top speed of 100mph and does 28 miles to the gallon. It costs £1,269.0s.10d. including Purchase Tax.

■ Families on the Netherhall Estate Leicester are being terrorised by a **vicious jackdaw** which has already attacked Merilyn Taylor (3), twice.

29 Thursday

Tiller girl Carole Lynn (21), is set to marry Henry Williams (22), who won £75,000 on the **football pools** last week and gave it all to his mother. Henry, who earns £7 a week, proposed and was accepted soon after he had been handed his pools cheque.

■ HOME ALONE: A policewoman called to a bungalow in Stoke-on-Trent, finds he back door open and two babies, a five-year-old and an 18-month-old, alone and eating crisps. The parents, who return at 1.30am, had gone to Blackpool for the day. They are fined £10 each, with £2.9s. costs, for neglecting the children.
. . . A general strike is called in CYPRUS. . .

30 Friday

James Dean (24) film star, lover of fast cars and famous for his roles as a teenage rebel, is **killed** in a road accident at Paso Rolles, California, USA. He will be buried in his native Indiana. He made an enormous impression in *East of Eden*, and *Rebel Without A Cause* (which is about to be shown in the USA). He had just finished filming *Giant*.

■ Dogs, bees and cows can still be sent by **special delivery** post, and leeches, bees and silkworms can go if they are properly packed. Animals can be posted if a suitable receptacle is provided, or if they're on a lead. However, drunks cannot be taken home by the GPO as they could be before the war.

OCTOBER

1 Saturday
Full Moon

The BBC starts experimental **colour TV** transmissions from Alexandra Palace at the end of normal programmes. All the viewer can see at the moment is patterns.
■ **Trout** are being removed from the River Lathkil, Derbyshire, as the river is drying up at their breeding ground near Bakewell.
Len Hutton, England's greatest batsman, is told he must rest for six months, and any manipulative or operative treatment must be indefinitely postponed.
. . . HURRICANE JACK hits the Caribbean and Mexico, killing 473 people . . .

2 Sunday

A man **climbs** the 320ft scaffolding tower around **Big Ben**, watched by crowds in Trafalgar Square. Within 10mins he's at the top. It takes an hour for the police to persuade him to come down. He is Louis Bradford (41), of Kingsworthy, Hants, a Canadian who once doubled for Gary Cooper, and he was protesting about the housing shortage.
. . . BORN: Phil Oakey, singer, songwriter and founder member of The Human League.

3 Monday

The Argentinian Government states that it will continue ex-President **Juan Peron**'s stand on the Falkland Islands (that they belong to Argentina).

■ **Sir John Harding** is sworn in as Governor and Commander-in-Chief of **Cyprus.**

■ **John Surtees** beats Geoff Duke at Silverstone and Brands Hatch to confirm his position as Britain's champion motorbike racer. He is unbeaten for three years.

Tuesday 4

American writer, Cleveland Amory (38) withdraws from collaborating with the **Duchess of Windsor** on her **memoirs.** Mr Amory, who is the second writer to try and work with the Duchess, said they could not agree. 'You cannot make the Duchess of Windsor into Rebecca of Sunnybrook Farm,' he said.

Wednesday 5

The **Inner Temple Hall**, London, is reopened. It was destroyed in 1941.

■ The **Tory Party conference** opens in Bournemouth tomorrow amid speculation that Anthony Eden is, at long last, going to reshuffle his cabinet.

■ **Gin** will go up by a 1d. a nip in pubs to offset the price increase of 9d. which brings the cost of a bottle to 34s.6d.

Thursday 6

The assistant director of the Meteorological Office, London, says that some of the rain that fell on London last night was experimental **artificial rain**.

■ High winds with **gusts** up to 71mph in the northwest—all flights are grounded at Speke Airport, Liverpool.

Friday 7

Soldiers remove an anti-tank **gun** from the top of one of the 20ft high arches of **Stonehenge** on Salisbury Plain.

■ Hitler's pilot, Hans Bauer, just released by

the USSR, confirms Eva Braun's and **Hitler's suicides** in 1945.

Saturday 8

A **Comet**, above, piloted by Captain John Cunningham, flies from Khartoum, Sudan, to Rome in 5hrs 20mins, a record for a commercial aircraft.

■ About 12,000 square miles of the **Punjab** is **flooded** by the river Ravi. Railway communications between India and Pakistan are at a standstill for five days. All the cotton and rice crops are damaged and 7,000 villages are inundated. Roads, canals, bridges and railway tracks are damaged. The government estimate the cost at £22.5 million.

Sunday 9

The **Royal Family** leave the parish church at Kinclaven, Perthshire and cross the River Tay in a fishing coble to return to Meikleour House, the home of the Marquis of Lansdowne, where they are spending the weekend.

■ After the third meeting between **Archbishop Makarios** of Cyprus, and **Sir John Harding**, the Governor, it is announced that they have been unable to reach an agreement on Cyprus.

■ Three men raid Turkish Baths in Jermyn Street, London, and get away with £7.

. . . Steve Ovett, athlete, born . .

Monday 10

The opening of the **Labour Party Conference** at Margate, where nationalization is the big issue.

■ Call-up **deferment** is being extended to all agricultural workers provided they can prove there would be a substantial loss of food production if the person concerned was called up.

11 Tuesday

Mr Clement Attlee (72), leader of the Labour Party, addresses the party conference in Margate, but refuses to be drawn on when he might resign. **Aneurin Bevan (left)** brings the conference alight with a rip-roaring speech on where responsibility lies for the lost general election.

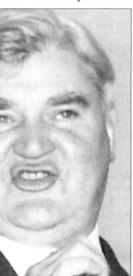

■ **Gordon Pirie** continues his battle with Emil Zatopek, the wonder Czech, winning the 10,000 metres at White City, avenging his defeat in Prague last month.

12 Wednesday

48 Lippizaner **horses** from the Spanish Riding School in Vienna, return from exile in Weis, Upper Austria. They were removed in March 1945 before the Red Army moved in, and kept safe under the patronage of General Patton. He also arranged for the stud to be moved back to Piber in Styria, Austria.

■ Composer **Ralph Vaughan Williams** celebrates his 83rd birthday by listening to his *Job, a Masque for Dancing*, performed by the BBC Symphony Orchestra, conducted by Sir Malcolm Sargent at the Royal Festival Hall.

■ Thick **fog** brings shipping and air services to a standstill.

13 Thursday

Thor Heyerdahl, the famous Norwegian explorer and author of *The Kon-Tiki Expedition*, sets sail on a new expedition to Easter Island to study the inhabitants and their way of life.

■ Flash the 10ft-long Australian **python** is

finally captured, putting an end to his 10 weeks of freedom in Cumnor, Berkshire, and the children of Cumnor are allowed out again.

14 Friday

British Summer Time ends. **Clocks** go **back** one hour.

■ Singer **Sir George Robey,** one of Britain's highest paid entertainers, gave most of his money away. He left so little when he died that his widow has decided not to apply for probate.

■ The Central Electric Authority announce that they propose to build their first two **nuclear power** stations at Bradwell at the mouth of the river Blackwater, Essex and at Berkeley on the river Severn in Gloucs.

■ William Connor (46), rescues a seagull impaled by its wing on a lightning conductor at the top of the 85ft flagpole at the Pierhead, Liverpool. The **seagull** is now recovering in the Liverpool RSPCA.

15 Saturday
New Moon

There is to be a **referendum** in Sweden on whether they should continue to drive on the left, like Britain, or on the right, like the rest of the Continent.

■ The Seventh Annual report of the Wildfowl Trust gives figures for the present status of the Ne Ne or **Hawaiian Goose**. Of an estimated world population of 70, 20 are at Slimbridge. In 1950 the world population was 40.

16 Sunday

Climbers in **Snowdonia** report the first snow of winter.

■ **Princess Elizabeth**'s Birthday Book has gone missing from Temple Meads Station, Bristol. 365 pages long, 56lbs in weight, packed in a blue suitcase, and containing the signatures of the Queen when she was 12, the Queen Mother and Princess Margaret, it was to go on show to raise funds for the Church of England Children's Society. But when the organiser called at

The multi-talented ALEC GUINNESS in *Kind Hearts and Coronets*, one of the many fine comedy films that put Ealing Studios, bought by the BBC, on the map

the left luggage office to pick it up, he was told it had already been collected.

17 Monday

■ The price of **cigarettes** is going up by 1/2d., and 1d. for the more expensive brands, for only the second time since 1939. A packet of10 will now cost 1s.10d.
■ Donald Campbell's boat, **Bluebird,** sinks in Lake Mead, Nevada, USA, after a test run, but is swiftly recovered.
■ Cold weather over most of the country. In London the temperature is only 39°F.

18 Tuesday

Dr Benjamin Mazar of the Hebrew University of Jerusalem announces the discovery of the Scroll of Lamech, a paraphrase and commentary on the Book of **Genesis** which has come to light with the deciphering of one of the Dead Sea Scrolls.

19 Wednesday

16,192 people visit the **Motor Show** in London on the first day. Amongst the new cars on display are the Jaguar 2.4, the Armstrong Siddey Sapphire 234, 2.3 litre, and the Citroën 2 litre. The favourite stands with visitors are MG, AC, Austin Healey, Morgan and Triumph.
■ Bombs wreck the post office in Nicosia, Cyprus.

■ Gales and **torrential rain** along the south and east coasts, Poole has 4ins rain in 24hrs, and Bournemouth 3.2ins. 1.3ins of rain falls on Stanmore, Middlesex in just 3 1/2hrs.

20 Thursday

The BBC buys **Ealing Film Studios**—the home of the 'Ealing Comedies' —*Kind Hearts and Coronets, Passport to Pimlico, The Lavender Hill Mob, The Man in the White Suit*—and many other successful films such as *Scott of the Antarctic, The Cruel Sea,* etc.
■ The BBC puts on an impressive demonstration of **colour television** at Alexandra Palace, avoiding the red and green faces that marred the first American showing five years ago.

21 Friday

The Dublin Post Office is to replace its 54 horse-drawn wagons and light letter vans with motors.
■ The **Archbishop of Canterbury** spends 45 mins with the Prime Minister, Sir Anthony Eden, at Downing Street. It is believed they discussed the possible marriage between Princess Margaret and Group Captain Peter Townsend.
■ Experiments carried out at Birkbeck College, London, prove that translation by **computer** is a real possibility.

22 Saturday

Dr Albert Schweitzer, OM, is awarded an honorary Ll.D at Cambridge.
■ Eighty US airmen volunteer to help Kent police and firemen search through a 40ft mound of debris when part of a cliff face and public stairway at Ramsgate **collapse.** There are no casualties.
■ Youths rioting in Nicosia are sprayed with coloured dye to mark them as troublemakers.

23 Sunday

It is announced that **Father Trevor Huddleston** of the Community of the Resurrection in Johannesburg, South Africa, will return to the UK in January. He is being recalled after 12yrs fighting apartheid in the slums and shanty towns surrounding Johannesburg.
■ British occupation forces troops leave Austria.
■ British film star, **Diana Dors**, real name Diana Fluck, is 24 today.

24 Monday

Five of the crew of a sinking French trawler, Henri Jacques, 25 tons, save themselves by jumping aboard the derelict British barge they collided with 12 miles north of Dieppe. The barge, the Will Everard, has been drifting in the Channel since last Friday.
■ Lord Chief Justice Goddard rules that selling a loaf of **bread** with a piece of string in it does not make it unfit for human consumption and quashes the conviction of Turner & Son Ltd of Nottingham.
■ The South African delegate to the **United Nations** walks out of the UN debate on apartheid, saying the UN was interfering in the internal politics of his country, contrary to its own charter.
■ The United Nations is 10 years old.

25 Tuesday

The NW Gas Board say that Manchester gasmen must give up wearing bowler hats and wear caps instead. The new uniform will be introduced over the next few months.
■ The Queen gives a **State banquet** for the President of Portugal and Madame Craveiro Lopes at Buckingham Palace.
. . . Glynis Barber, actress, born.

26 Wednesday

Uproar in the House of Commons as R A Butler, the Chancellor of the Exchequer announces increased Purchase Tax on clothing, footwear, kitchen and household goods, and furniture in his autumn budget.
■ The Birthday Book containing the signatures of the Queen when she was 12, the Queen Mother and Princess Margaret, which was lost at Temple Meads Station, Bristol, last week (see October 16), turns up at the George and Railway Hotel, Bristol.
■ **The Village Voice**, the famous underground American newspaper, is launched. Novelist **Norman Mailer** is one of the backers.
■ **State of Emergency** declared in Cyprus.

27 Thursday

Icelandic writer, Halldor Laxness wins the **Nobel Prize** for Literature.
■ The State of **Utah**, USA, files **polygamy** charges against Loris Kelch (41), who is the father of 31 children under the age of 18. He admits cohabiting with his five 'wives' since he was released from prison in 1947.
■ **Sheila van Damm,** Britain's leading woman motor racing driver and European Rally Champion, is to retire from motor rac-

ing to help her father, Vivian van Damm, run the Windmill Theatre, but she will compete in the Monte Carlo Rally first.

28 Friday

Offa's Dyke, which runs 168 miles from north to south Wales, is to be a public foot-path .
■ British troops in **Cyprus** are put on wartime footing for a three-month period.
■ The best-tailored picket lines in history are outside five Cadillac motor showrooms in Los Angeles, California. The salesmen, who earn up to £130 commission a week, are striking for more job security, and hail prospective customers with, 'Don't be a cad and buy a Cad'.
■ Ice and **snow** brings traffic to a crawl in NE Scotland.

29 Saturday

Scientists are testing an **anti-smog** bottle, like the familiar kitchen smell killer. Strips of special detector paper are provided with each bottle and the paper turns red if the atmosphere is too smoggy; blue if too much ammonia is coming out of the bottle, and greenish-yellow when the smog-killer is doing its job properly.
■ The RSPCA asks walkers and ramblers in the Peak District National Park to look out for an Australian wallaby which is at large.

30 Sunday

The whooping **cranes** arrive at their wintering grounds, a wildlife sanctuary at Matagorda, Texas, having defeated the US airforce who wanted to take over part of their wintering ground for a bombing range. Thirteen cranes have made the annual 2,000 mile flight from NW Canada.

31 Monday
Full Moon

Princess Margaret, in a dramatic announcement from Clarence House, tells

the world, 'I would like it to be known that I have decided not to marry Group Captain Peter Townsend.' When told of the Princess's statement the Primus of the Episcopal Church in Scotland replied, 'Thank God for that. One is very thankful that her sense of duty has pre-vailed, for quite obviously this is a matter of very great importance to the moral standards of the country.' (See panel on page 80).
■ The Queen and the Duke of Edinburgh attend the Royal Command Film Performance of Alfred Hitchcock's *To Catch A Thief*, starring **Cary Grant** and **Grace Kelly**. Before the film they meet **Gina Lollobrigida, Ava Gardner, Peter Ustinov** and **Diana Dors**, whose dress has the lowest neckline ever seen at a Royal film performance.

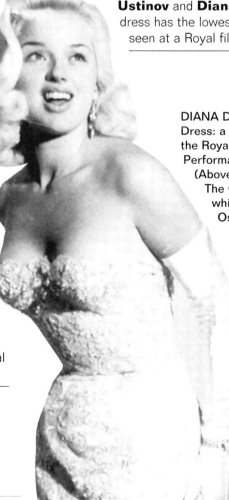

DIANA DORS and That Dress: a star attraction at the Royal Command Film Performance.
(Above) Grace Kelly, in The Country Girl, for which she won an Oscar this year.

STORY OF THE YEAR—PRINCESS MA

Princess Margaret ends weeks of press speculation about the possibility of her marrying Group Captain Peter Townsend with her announcement on October 31. The public first became aware of the romance between the princess and the handsome equerry in July 1953, when the group captain was suddenly posted to Brussels as Air Attache, instead of accompanying the princess and her mother on their tour of Africa. They were not to meet again for 2 years and 3 months.

GROUP CAPT. Peter Townsend in his RAF days (left), and above, in his role as a Royal Equerry with Princess Margaret.

-ARET AND GROUP CAPT TOWNSEND

oup Capt. Townsend's wife and son see him off
ngagement with the princess.

1 Tuesday

Intense interest throughout the world in the story of Princess Margaret and Group Captain Peter Townsend. The British press is almost unanimous in its view that the princess has taken the right decision, and has undone much of the harm done by Edward VIII and Mrs Simpson.

■ The **Duke of Edinburgh** unveils an astronomical clock in York Minster in remembrance of the World War II airmen who died flying from bases in Yorkshire, Northumberland and Durham.

■ Villagers in south Westmorland have green **water** coming out of their taps. Marker dye from a US Superfortress, which crashed near Tarnhouse reservoir, Lupton, last week, has leaked into the water supply.

2 Wednesday

More anti-British **riots** in Cyprus.

■ A thin and starving **black cat** has been found in a crate containing unassembled motor car parts in Durban, S Africa. It is believed that the cat was sealed in the crate at Cowley, Oxford. The manager of the plant says that the cat must have lived in the crate for three months without food or water.

■ **Sir Thomas Beecham**, who is conducting the Hallé Orchestra for the first time in 16 years, receives a standing ovation from the capacity audience at Manchester's Free Trade Hall.

3 Thursday

The Foreign Minister of the Netherlands, in a speech at the Foreign Press Association, speaks of the need for Europe to cooperate

or even unite in order to provide a home market.

■ **General Peron**, ex-President of Argentina, leaves Paraguay for Nicaragua, where he is thought to be a possible resident in exile.

■ The British Museum acquires the *Rous Roll*—the famous 15th-century work of a chantry priest which celebrates the lives and deeds of all holders of the earldom of Warwick from 1484 backwards to mythical times.

4 Friday

Group Captain Peter Townsend returns to Brussels to resume his duties as Air Attaché.

■ The price of Four Square **cigarettes** is raised by a penny to 3s.8d. for 20.

■ The television public in Great Britain in the period June-September is approximately 13 million—a rise of three million on the same period last year.

■ A herd of **cattle** strays onto the West Coast line at Garstang, north of Preston. 15 trains are held up, the line is closed for two hours, and farmer John Kellett of Galgate, who lost five heifers and two bullocks, estimates his loss at £400.

5 Saturday

Maurice Utrillo (71), **pictured,** the French painter best known for his Paris street scenes, dies at his home in Dax.

■ Police are looking for more than 50 road signs, valued at more than £300, that have been removed from roads in the western part of Leicestershire.

6 Sunday

The Americans retain the **Ryder Cup**, beat-

ing the British team of Dai Rees (capt), Ken Bousfield, Harry Bradshaw, Harry Weetman, Eric Brown and Christie O'Connor at Thunderbird Ranch, California.
■ NBC announce that by next autumn, they will be broadcasting 70hrs of colour television a week in the USA.
■ Chinese troops cross the border into **Tibet.**

7 Monday

Real farmhouse cheese is back on the market again.
■ **Transworld Airlines** is now operating the first regular air service between London and Los Angeles, with one stop in New York. The plane leaves London at 10.10pm on Fridays, and passengers disembark at Burbank, Los Angeles, 22hrs and 23mins flying time later.
■ The Royal Variety Performance: on the bill are The Crazy Gang, the Tiller Girls, Channing Pollock, Ruby Murray, the cast of Kismet and Johnnie Ray. The compere is Tommy Trinder.

8 Tuesday

Plans are announced for the building of six new British liners—four for the Royal Mail Line, and two for the Australian service of P&O.
■ The 2,000th edition of 'Mrs Dale's Diary' is broadcast this afternoon.

9 Wednesday

Film star **Rock Hudson**, right, who vowed he would not get married until he was 30, ties the knot with **Phyllis Gates**, secretary to Rock's agent, just eight days before his 30th birthday.
■ A list of **baby-sitters** in Liverpool is being compiled. The Bishop of Liverpool, Dr

Martin, wants to strengthen the bonds of family unity and security, and enable the babies' mothers to attend church services.
■ It's the end of the **herring** season—the worst on record.

10 Thursday

Prime Minister **Sir Anthony Eden** offers to help in the Arab-Israeli dispute.
■ In the House of Commons, Colonel Marcus Lipton, MP (Labour), withdraws the allegations he made against Mr H A R **Philby** that he was the 'Third Man' who warned **Burgess** and **Maclean** that they were under surveillance.

11 Friday
Dominion Day, New Zealand

President Eisenhower, looking cheerful but frail, returns to Washington after seven weeks in hospital in Denver recovering from a heart attack. Nine brass bands, thousands of soldiers and 200,000 people line the streets.
■ Freddy Leyland, a chargehand at the Fibre Glass Works, St Helen's, Lancs, finds £8,000 in bags of **silver** marked 'Royal Mint', in a container van. The van was carrying money to a St Helen's bank, and got shunted into the glass fibre yard instead.

12 Saturday

Britain enters the **scooter** race. At the Cycle and Motor Show at Earls Court, London, BSA launches two models— the Beeza, a luxury scooter selling for £204.12s., including purchase tax, which has a 198cc four-stroke engine, 4-speed gears, sprung suspension and an electric starter, and the Dandy, £74.8s, a lightweight model, which does 200 miles per gallon and has a speed of about 40mph.

13 Sunday

Of the 194 cars that set out on the **London-Brighton run**, 187 were there on time. The first car to reach Brighton was a 1900 New Orleans, and the last, with 20secs to spare, a 1902 Peugeot, that had to be pushed most of the last five miles because its engine had stopped.

■ US Federal Tax Authorities impound a French **racehorse,** Mahan, because his owner, who has racing establishments in both France and the USA, is alleged to owe the government $106,000.

14 Monday
New Moon

The **Duke of Cornwall**, pictured, is seven today.

■ **Ruby M Ayres** (72), whose romantic novels have been best-sellers for more than 50 years, dies at a nursing home in Weybridge, Surrey. She wrote more than 150 love stories, and about nine million copies of her books have been sold. At the height of her fame, it was estimated that her royalties were around £20,000 a year.

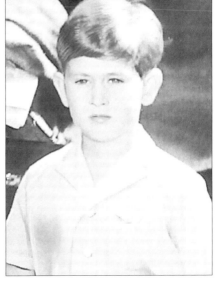

15 Tuesday

Dashing film actor **Errol Flynn**, star of many swashbuckling roles, Robin Hood, The Master of Ballantrae, etc. where his swordplay won the day, is challenged to a bout of foils with the Brighton & Hove Fencing Club. He cables back declining the challenge saying that he can't fence, he can only fake it.

■ The advance party of the Trans-Antarctic Expedition, led by **Sir Vivian Fuchs** and **Sir Edmund Hillary**, sets sail from London on MV Theron. The 24 huskies they are taking with them prove to be the star attraction.

■ In Chicago, **Adlai Stevenson** announces that he will stand for the democratic nomination for the presidency.

16 Wednesday

The vice president of the Institute of Journalists defends the **Press** in the Princess Margaret affair. He feels that, 'most, if not all, of the hullabaloo could have been avoided if, at the beginning, the co-operation of the press had been sought.'

■ The morning **programmes** on commercial television's London stations are getting such small audiences that they may be scrapped.

■ **Donald Campbell** breaks his own world water-speed record by 14mph on Lake Mead, Nevada, USA. Bluebird reaches 216.2mph.

17 Thursday

A Government report published today recommends that top **civil servants** should get a £30 a week pay rise, bringing their salaries to £6,000pa— £500pa more than their political masters. It also suggests a 5mins tea break every afternoon, and an hour for lunch instead of the present 45mins.

■ A Finnish couple are married on a boat in the international waters off Bridlington, Yorks, because the Finnish minister in Britain has not yet received his certificate to marry people in Britain.

■ Angelesey is the first authority in Britain to introduce fluoride into the water supply.

■ Field Marshal Lord **Montgomery** celebrates his 68th birthday.

18 Friday

Opera singer **Maria Callas**, left, leaves the USA for Italy after an amazing scene at Chicago's civic Opera House, where she has been singing the title role in Madame Butterfly. Eight men try to serve her with summonses issued on behalf of a New York lawyer, who claims he has a contract entitling him to 10% of Mme Callas's earnings.

IF YOU WANT TO GET AHEAD . . .

. . . and there are plenty of imaginative millinery choices judging by the many new creations displayed on the catwalks, at Royal Ascot (left), and in the fashion houses this year.

■ Seventy-eight oil-covered **swans** from the River Thames in Oxford are being treated by the RSPCA at Putney.

19 Saturday

Hampstead Council workers are searching the rubbish dump for £2,000 worth of jewellery which the owner had hidden in a purse in a wastepaper basket. She then found that the domestic staff had thrown the contents into the dustbin.

■ The **Royal Court Theatre**, Sloane Square, London, is bought by the English Stage Company, which plans to begin productions next spring.

■ **Arthur Murray**, the man who taught America to dance, is opening a chain of schools in Britain. A course costs from 59gns —or you can become a life member by paying 2,000 guineas for 1,200 dancing hours.

20 Saturday

BBC television is inundated with angry telephone calls while the panel of *The Brains Trust* are still in the process of answering the question, 'At what age should children not be encouraged to believe in Father Christmas?' The calls are mostly from fathers complaining that the question has spoilt Christmas for their families.

21 Monday

The Vatican says that **Pope Pius XII** saw a vision of Christ at the climax of a recent illness and from that moment started to get better.

■ An American inventor has developed a revolutionary new **typewriter** which, he claims, will increase the output of the average typist by 35%. He has placed the letters that are most commonly used closest to the most active fingers.

22 Tuesday

The manager of the Standard Bank of South Africa in Northumberland Avenue, London, receives a small brown parcel containing two phials in the post this morning. He takes them to the police who identify them as strychnine and cyanide. There is enough **poison** in the phials to kill 300 people. The police advise him to check the names of people with overdrafts.

■ In Cyprus, the police use tear-gas to quell **riots** in Nicosia and Larnaca.

23 Wednesday

The lady trombone players in **Ivy Benson**'s famous band get more proposals of marriage than the players of any other instrument. But even though they earn £12-£25 a week, and the trombone takes a long time to learn, they usually leave the band when they get married.

■ Leaders of the TUC warn that if **wages** keep rising without corresponding increases in output, unemployment will follow. Nearly all 35 members of the TUC's top leadership are currently negotiating new wage claims.

THOUSANDS OF

MILLIONS

of road miles have proved it

The "Quality First"

MORRIS
MINOR

is still the world's biggest small car buy

REMEMBER:—Quality and dependability are guaranteed by the B.M.C. Used-Car Warranty and you are certain of a good deal when you sell.

MORRIS MOTORS LTD., COWLEY, OXFORD.
London Distributors: Morris House, Berkeley Sq.,W.1
Overseas Business: Nuffield Exports Ltd. Oxford
& 41 Piccadilly, London, W.1.

■ The BBC says it will start an experimental **Schools** TV broadcasting service in 1957.

24 Thursday

ITV cuts the culture. Whenever a serious programme appears on ITV, thousands of viewers are turning off. So, off to early evening or late at night go the Hallé Orchestra concerts with Sir John Barbirolli, the discussion programme 'Foreign Press Club', and the dog programme 'Man's Best Friend'.

. . . IAN BOTHAM, cricketer, is born in Cheshire. . .

■ Australia is waging war on **grasshoppers.** A Dakota aircraft makes nine strikes against targets on the Murray River. The swarms cover 110 square miles and are the greatest threat to 1,500,000 acres of agricultural land since the swarms of 1943. Each flight of the Dakota covers 350 acres.

25 Friday

Rear-Admiral **William Byrd** (67) joins the vanguard of his expedition to **Antarctica.** He has been given virtually a free hand in political, scientific, legislative and operational aspects of the American Antarctic programme. Admiral Byrd says that a permanent US base at the South Pole could have high strategic value if the Panama Canal is ever destroyed.

■ **King Haakon** of Norway celebrates the 50th anniversary of his arrival in Norway from Denmark (he acceded to the Norwegian throne when Norway gained its independence from Sweden in 1905). He has been in hospital for five months with a fractured thigh.

26 Saturday

The stairway gas lamps at Stechford Station, Birmingham, are removed and 26 electric lights put in for the arrival of the **Queen** and the **Duke of Edinburgh** at the beginning of their tour of the Midlands. When the Royals have gone, the gas lamps are put back.

■ Russia sets off its biggest hydrogen bomb yet—the equivalent to a million tons of TNT.

AN UNDERCOVER STORY . . .

What the well-dressed woman is wearing under her haute couture this year . . .

27 Sunday

Germany's ex-arms king **Alfred Krupp** gives a welcome home party for his brother, who has returned from a Russian labour camp. He invites 640 guests to his 300-roomed villa, and each of them receives a silver cigarette lighter. During the afternoon the guests tour the factory, which is now producing locomotives and false teeth.

28 Monday

Offers from five foreign zoos have been received for Charles, the **elephant** threatened with destruction because of the imminent closure of Craigend Castle Zoo, Glasgow.
■ **Comet III** flies more than 3,300 miles non-stop over the UK, in 7hrs 22mins.

29 Tuesday
Full Moon

Film producer **Herbert Wilcox**'s current

film *I Have a Teenage Daughter*, starring Kenneth Haigh and Sylvia Sims, is a gold-mine of current jive talk— 'Cool it, Daddy', 'Go man, go!', 'This place is jumping', 'Weave, Steve', 'Get with it, chick'. And, if you want to say yes when asked to dance, the only hip reply is, 'OK creep, let's crawl'.

30 Wednesday
St Andrew's Day

240 **schoolchildren** in Leek, Staffs, go on **strike** when their headmaster cancels their Christmas party. He says only a few of the pupils attend the school's annual festival services at Leek Parish Church and the ban results from 'disloyalty to the school'.
■ The first **floodlit football** match is played at Wembley between England and Spain.
■ Twenty counties in the south and west of England are blanketed in **fog.** In central London it is almost dark by mid-afternoon. There are no flights in or out of airports for six hours.

DECEMBER

1 Thursday

From March next year there will no longer be **Third Class** railway coaches on trains, just First Class and the rest, to bring Britain into line with the rest of Europe, say the Transport Commission.
■ New **pennies** and halfpennies being minted for Guernsey have a new design with a Guernsey cow on the obverse.

2 Friday

The Duchess of Windsor has selected a title for her autobiography—*The Heart has its Reasons*.
■ 2,179 pigeons compete at the **World Pigeon Show** in the Royal Horticultural Halls, London. Best Bird of Show is Mollie (2), who belongs to Welsh miner Trevor Parker.
■ RAIL CRASH: Twelve people die and 45

are injured when the 11.12pm from Waterloo to Windsor bursts into flames after running into a goods train 200 yards from Barnes Station.

3 Saturday

The Czech embassy in London complains to the Foreign Office about the presence of **microphones** in the walls of their building.
■ Miners James and Paul Corrigan of Chirk, Denbighshire, Wales, sleep in a room haunted by a nun, a nurse and a bishop. Despite the efforts of priests and professional ghost hunters, they will not go away. The Council says no ghosts are allowed in council houses and has given the Corrigans notice to quit.
■ A Swedish expert says that the **Coronation chair** is in a state of decay.

4 Sunday

Fog closes airports in the south of England.
■ Thousands of blacks **boycott** the bus company in protest at the fine of $14 imposed on Rosa Parks (42), who last Thursday ignored a bus driver's order to move to the back of the bus as required by local race laws in Montgomery, Alabama, USA.

5 Monday

The BBC claims victory in the first round of its struggle with commercial **television.** During the first eight weeks, 56% of adult viewers with a choice watched BBC and 44% watched ITV.
■ The Comet III arrives in Sydney from London in 24hrs 23mins, the record for a commercial aircraft. 20,000 people turn up to greet it on arrival.
■ A weather plane leaves the US Air Force base nr.Warrington, Cheshire, for the North Pole, carrying 2,000 letters for Santa Claus. The crew will drop the letters at the **North Pole**.

6 Tuesday

One of **Napoleon's teeth**, a lock of his

hair and the order of the Legion d'Honneur which he wore at Waterloo, are sold at Sotheby's for £38.

■ Miners at the East Pit, Gwaun-cae-Gurwen, Glam, are not allowed to use the new pit-head **baths** until output increases.

■ The Forestry Commission, in its drive against the **grey squirrel**, has doubled the rate to 2s. per tail presented to pest officers.

■ The government of Cyprus imposes a fine of £2,000 on the people of the village of Lefkoniko as punishment for the destruction of the post office by schoolboys.

■ The 2d. minimum fare on London **buses** is raised to 2 1/2d.

7 Wednesday

Durham County Water Board **rations** 240,000 consumers, who have to get water from street taps turned on for only two hours a day. Durham has had a drought since July.

■ **Clement Attlee** (72) resigns as leader of the Labour party, and becomes an Earl.

■ 98 'poor and industrious' old people queue at Bolton Parish Church to receive parcels of winter clothes and a 2lb loaf—the gift of a 126-year-old charity founded by Dr John Popplewell.

■ The Minister of Fuel and Power, Geoffrey Lloyd, says Britain is now the most important **oil refining** country in western Europe. In some industries such as steel, glass and ceramics, oil is already replacing coal as a power source.

8 Thursday

Farm workers get an increase of 8s. a week to bring their minimum weekly **wage** to £6.15s.

■ **Jean Sibelius**, above, the Finnish composer noted particularly for his tone poem Finlandia and Valse Triste, celebrates his 90th birthday. At a celebratory concert at the Royal Festival Hall, Sir Thomas Beecham is presented with the Finnish Order of the White Rose in appreciation of his work in spreading the knowledge or Sibelius's music.

9 Friday

Harold Wilson, the Labour MP for Huyton, asks on a point of order whether it would not be possible for the Sergeant of Arms to acquire a new hat for the raising of points of order in a division. The top hat he is wearing is ancient and threadbare.

■ The Gas and Electricity Councils announce that they will no longer rent out cookers.

■ The last-ever Ealing Comedy, *The Ladykillers*, starring **Alec Guinness**, opens at the Odeon, Leicester Square.

■ **Sugar Ray Robinson** knocks out Carl Olson to regain the World Middleweight Boxing title.

■ Yvonne Sugden (16) wins the British Women's **Figure Skating** championship at Streatham Ice Rink for the third year in succession.

10 Saturday

The Secretary of the National Federation of Felt Hat manufacturers offers to provide a new **top hat** to replace the 'deplorable and tatty' one currently used by MPs to raise a point of order, partly as a thank-you for reducing the tax on hats.

■ The state of Georgia, USA, will not enforce **integration,** says the Attorney General, and they will withhold state aid from integrated schools.

■ Two men break into a church in Cairo and steal a gold **crown** from the statue of Our Lady of Fatima. The Egyptian police arrest one of them, but fail to catch the one with the crown.

11 Sunday

The first **boy bishop** of Canvey is enthroned at St Katherine's Church on the island, to hold office until December 28. He is Antony Phillips (12), and his duties will include conducting the Sunday evening services at St Nicholas's Guild.

■ **Prayers for rain** are offered in all

HELLO . . .

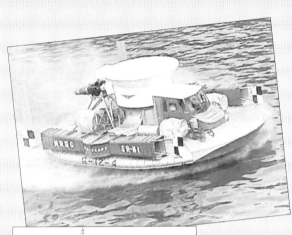

The Hovercraft
Hugh Gaitskell as leader of the Labour Party
Blue jeans
The Vickers Valiant
Earrings for Dogs
Killer smog
USS Nautilus
A magnetic tape recorder for television
Commercial television
The Flying Bedstead
The Rome Underground
Industrial quality synthetic diamonds
The aircraft carrier Ark Royal
Equal pay for women teachers and members of the civil service
Salk anti-polio vaccine
VHF broadcasting
Parking meters
The Warsaw Pact
Disneyland
National Library of Wales
Annigoni's portrait of the Queen
The Wimpy Bar
Pakistan, an independent republic within the Commonwealth
Wave of immigrants from the West Indies

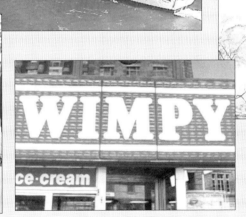

Greetings: (from top), the hovercraft, USS Nautilus, Ark Royal, Hugh Gaitskell, Caribbean immigrants and the Wimpy Bar

AND GOODBYE . . .

No longer with us: (left) Sir Alexander Fleming; and (clockwise from below left): Annette Mills; Albert Einstein; James Dean; Maurice Utrillo, as symbolised by one of his paintings; and Ealing Studios, home of the famous comedy films

Sen. Joe McCarthy's Un-American Activities Committee
Annette Mills, of Muffin The Mule fame
The Piltdown Man
Segregation in schools in the southern states of the USA
The *Chicago Tribune*'s simplified spelling
HMS Vanguard, The Royal Navy's only active-service battleship
Grace Archer — sacrificed on the altar of commercial television
Albert Einstein
Sir Alexander Fleming
James Dean
Thomas Mann
Maurice Utrillo
Fernand Leger
Ealing comedies
Ruby M Ayres
500 emigrants a week on their way to Australia

churches in County Durham. Mr C F Grey, MP, joins the prayers, as he has had no reply from the Air Ministry to his request for a rainmaker.

12 Monday

Radio listeners in County Durham telephone the police to say they are receiving messages on their radios from police headquarters to patrol cars. A spokesman for the police says it is due to the new VHF sets, and security is not in danger.
■ The **USA evacuates** its consulate in Hanoi, North Vietnam.
■ Snow, ice, and fog cause problems for motorists in Scotland and the north of England.

13 Tuesday

Water rationing in County Durham (they have only 10 days' supply for their 500,000 consumers), is hindered by 15° of frost. When inspectors turn on the first of nearly 700 standpipes, they find many of them are frozen.
■ **Christopher Cockerell (left)** is granted the patent on his prototype **Hovercraft.**
■ Only three tram routes remain in Liverpool. A new bus terminal opens today.

14 Wednesday

New Moon

Local clergymen complain about the Merseyside and North Wales Electricity Board **advertisement** showing life-size figures of the Three Wise Men at the crib offering a washing machine, a cooker and a refrigerator as gifts, and it is withdrawn.
■ **Hugh Gaitskell** (49) becomes leader of the Labour Party by 157 votes to Aneurin

"You waiting for glasses too, chum?"

Bevan's 70 and Herbert Morrison's 40. **Herbert Morrison** resigns as deputy.

15 Thursday

King Frederick of Denmark starts Jen Olsen's amazing world **clock** which has been called the Danish 8th Wonder of the World. It tells the time in various ways for different latitudes; shows the phases of the moon; shows movable feasts (like Easter), and has a calendar for 570,000 years. It indicates when eclipses of the sun and moon will take place, and on which day any date within the next 4,000 years will fall. It is claimed that the clock will lose only 1sec in a thousand years. It has 15,000 hand-made parts and 445 cogwheels. The slowest-turning wheel, to measure equinoxes, would have taken 26,000 years to complete a revolution, so builders put in only a 1/4 wheel — enough for 6,000 years.
■ Dense **fog,** gales, snow and floods all over Britain. In County Durham, visibility on many roads is nil. Gusts of wind up to 94mph are recorded in Orkney.

16 Friday

British Rail apologises to passengers on the 8pm from Derby to Nottingham, who have to wait 15mins at Sawley Junction for the guard to catch up with them. When he waved his signal lamp at Derby he noticed there was something wrong with it and stopped to examine it. The train went off and he had to walk to Sawley Junction to catch it.
■ London **Heathrow** opens its new terminal buildings, and establishes itself as the world's biggest international airport.
■ Author and humorist **P G Wodehouse** becomes an American citizen in a ceremony at Riverhead, New York, USA.

17 Saturday

London is to get a new-look **taxi,** if the

police give their approval. It has a stream-lined bonnet, a giant luggage compartment in the rear and luxury bench-type seats. The driver is more comfortable, too, with a heater, a demister, and no draughts because the old open luggage carrier is now enclosed.
■ The Daily Mirror dubs Swedish actress **Anita Ekberg** (24), below, 'Shape of the Year'.

18 Sunday

Britain and America offer Egypt a first instalment of $70 million to finance the building of the Aswan High Dam on the river Nile.
■ The **Comet III** airliner sets a new record of 3hr 55mins for the 2,182 mile flight from Vancouver to Toronto, an average 560mph.

19 Monday

Twenty widows and spinsters of Dethwick, Lea & Holloway, Derbs, are the last to benefit from Alleyne's **Charity,** set up 300yrs ago to give each of them a loaf at Christmas. The village baker finds it a nuisance to bake 20 sixpenny loaves, and next year it has been decided to give the entire 10s. to one of the oldest residents in the parish.
■ Questions are asked in the House about the 15 obsolete British Valentine **tanks** being loaded on an Egyptian ship in Antwerp. There is an embargo on arms sales to Israel and Egypt.

20 Tuesday

Manchester gets its first **snow** of the winter. By 2am there is almost 2ins in the suburbs.
■ 5,000 motorists in the City of London get a Christmas card from the Commissioner of Police urging them to lock their parcels out of sight and not give thieves an open invitation to steal their property.
■ Sweeping Cabinet changes see R A

Butler become Lord Privy Seal, Harold Macmillan move to the Treasury, **Selwyn Lloyd** (right) become Foreign Secretary, **Lord Monckton** Minister of Defence, and **Iain Macleod** Minister of Labour.

21 Wednesday

Cardiff is selected by the majority of Welsh people and the government as the capital of Wales.

22 Thursday

On the first night of his telephone service at Hull, N Yorks, **Santa Claus** has 6,000 calls. One of the calls comes from Guernsey, several from Northern Ireland and some from Manchester street telephone boxes.
■ Two weather ships in the Atlantic, 300 miles west of the Irish coast, are still waiting for Santa's helicopter drop, but the snow makes it too dangerous to take off.

23 Friday

100 deprived British **children** visit the US Air Force station at Cranage, Cheshire, for the Christmas party of a lifetime. Each child is met by an American airman. They have turkey and ice cream, a Wild West film show, and a visit from Father Christmas. American forces at the base raised £400 for presents.

24 Saturday
CHRISTMAS EVE

Alistair Cooke reports from America on Christmas in New York. One of the big department store's windows are such an essential part of Christmas that the traffic is re-routed so that children can safely wander around looking at them.This year depicts the Christmas scene in a familiar New York setting: The Wise Men at Grand Central Station, Mary and Joseph huddled under Brooklyn Bridge, and the birth of Jesus taking place in an Eastside hovel.
■ The Inspector General of the Royal

FACES OF THE YEAR

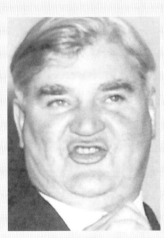

Top row (from Left):
Billy Graham, Premier Bulganin, Donald Campbell, Winston Churchill, Clement Attlee, Rosa Parks, Sir Anthony Eden, Bill Haley.

Centre:
Ruth Ellis, Johnnie Ray, Princess Margaret, Gp Capt. Peter Townsend, Jimmy Young, Dr Jonas Salk, Nikita Khruschev, Sheila Van Damm.

Bottom:
Nye Bevan, Lady Docker, Archbishop Makarios, John Surtees, Juan Peron, Angela Mortimer

Ulster Constabulary receives an unwelcome Christmas gift of mince pies laced with cyanide.

■ Charlie (23), Craigend Castle Zoo's unwanted **elephant,** is offered a home at one of Mr Butlin's holiday camps. Charlie can look forward to a Christmas dinner of 3 cases of apples, 1/2 case of bananas, 1/4 case of oranges and 1cwt of carrots. His usual diet costs £20 a week.

25 Sunday
CHRISTMAS DAY

More than 700 million letters and cards are posted this **Christmas.** This includes 150,000 cards posted on Christmas Eve to the temporary workers who helped Post Office Staff for the last two weeks.

26 Monday
BOXING DAY

During a performance at the Davis Theatre, Croydon, three **lions escape** from their cage, but they are swiftly rounded up before they can do any harm.

27 Tuesday

More than 420 extra **trains** are put on to carry Christmas holidaymakers back home. BEA put on nearly 100 extra flights for servicemen to get back to Germany, and 52 extra domestic flights.

■ Samples of Scottish **worms** are being sent to an Ohio firm of fish bait suppliers by two men anxious to secure an order for 10,000 worms. If anyone cares to send them samples, they need earthworms 8-10ins long.

28 Wednesday

The second national **Boat Show** opens at Olympia with more than 170 boats, dinghies and cruisers. The show is opened with the presentation to Donald Campbell of his cer-

tificate for the world water-speed record. A big attraction is a replica of the *Mayflower*, which is being built in Brixham to repeat the Pilgrim Fathers' voyage of 1620.

■ An American **soldier** in Bussac, France, turns on the tap in the shower and gets white wine instead of water. The residents of Bussac have to buy water when the wells are low, and the same tankers are sometimes used to transport wine.

29 Thursday
Full Moon

A **sheep,** stuck on a ledge in a stone quarry in Derbyshire, is finally rescued when a police sergeant lassoes it and lowers it 90ft into the arms of an RSPCA inspector.

30 Friday

Accles and Pollock of Oldbury, are employing **pensioners** as office boys because of the shortage of staff caused by the raising of the school leaving age and national service. They work half a day, alternate mornings and afternoons, and earn about £2 a week.

■ Film star **Gregory Peck** marries French journalist, Veronique Passani (23), after the longest interview of his life. Veronique was sent to interview him three years ago for a magazine.

31 Saturday

British **migration** to **Australia** is the highest for three years. About 500 a week are leaving on assisted passages, and Australia House says that more than 96% of all Australia's 1955 immigrants are settled permanently.

■ Runner **Gordon Pirie** and horsewoman **Pat Smythe** are elected sportsman and sportswoman of the year.

Who eats *who* in the Desert?

Andrew Campbell

W
FRANKLIN WATTS
LONDON•SYDNEY

KT-376-417

PROJECT LOAN

Designer: Cali Roberts
Editor: Constance Novis
Art Director: Peter Scoulding
Editor-in-Chief: John C. Miles
Picture Research: Diana Morris
Artwork: Ian Thompson

© 2005 Franklin Watts

First published in 2005
by Franklin Watts
96 Leonard Street
London
EC2A 4XD

Franklin Watts Australia
45-51 Huntley Street
Alexandria
NSW 2015

ISBN 0 7496 6079 1

A CIP catalogue record for this book is
available from the British Library.

Printed in Times Offset Malaysia

Dewey classification number: 577.54

PICTURE CREDITS

John Calcalosi/Still Pictures: 9, 16bl, 21, 24
Brian Cushing/Ecoscene: 14
Michele Depraz/Still Pictures: 12
Nigel J Dennis/Still Pictures: 27
Xavier Eichaker/Still Pictures: 6, 15, 17
M & P Fogden/FLPA: 7
Klein/Hubert/Still Pictures: 4b
Wayne Lawler/Ecoscene: 18, 19
Wyman Meinzer/Still Pictures: front cover, 1, 22
C. Allan Morgan/Still Pictures: 25
Michael Rauch/Still Pictures: 13
Ed Reschke/Still Pictures: 11
Francois Sauveny/Still Pictures: 26
Roland Seitre/Still Pictures: 8
Raoul Slater/WWI/Still Pictures: 10
Tom Vezo/Still Pictures: 20
Gordon Wiltsie/Still Pictures: 5t, 16tr
Gunter Ziesler/Still Pictures: 23

*Every attempt has been made to clear copyright. Should
there be any inadvertent omission please apply to the
publisher for rectification.*

Note to parents and teachers
Every effort has been made by the Publishers to ensure
that the websites in this book are suitable for children,
that they are of the highest educational value, and that
they contain no inappropriate or offensive material.
However, because of the nature of the Internet, it is
impossible to guarantee that the contents of these sites
will not be altered. We strongly advise that Internet
access is supervised by a responsible adult.

Contents

Life in the desert

Deserts are extreme places. They can be very hot during the day and very cold at night. They can also be very dry. In South America's Atacama Desert, for example, it only rained four times in one hundred years.

Extreme landscapes

The landscape of the desert is affected by the great range of temperatures. Very few plants can survive in such a wide range of hot, dry and cold conditions. Some landscapes are simply made up of endless sand dunes or large rocks. Only a few types of grass, trees or bushes can be found growing there.

Yummy!

The camel spider lives in deserts around the world and can grow up to 15 cm long. It likes to catch and eat lizards and small birds.

Survival

Because deserts are such extreme places, the plants, animals and people that live there have to depend on each other in order to survive.

In the Sahara Desert in Africa – the largest desert on Earth – goats survive by eating such grasses as are available. In turn, people living there, known as Bedouins, drink goats' milk.

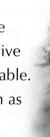

We're in the chain!

Nomads are people who have survived in deserts for thousands of years. In Africa, nomads such as the Bedouin people keep herds of goats and camels, which they rely on for milk and meat.

Habitats and food chains

All organisms (living things) require a place to live where they can find everything necessary for survival. This place is known as a habitat. Within every habitat exist food chains. These are simple lists showing the links between who eats what, or whom. By looking at a food chain you can see how each part of the chain helps to keep the next part alive.

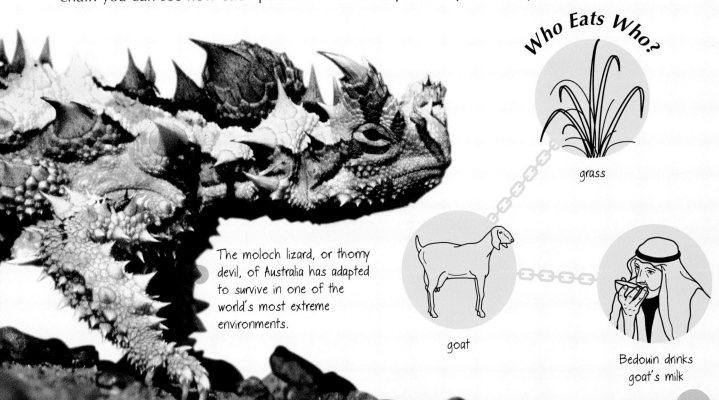

The moloch lizard, or thorny devil, of Australia has adapted to survive in one of the world's most extreme environments.

Who Eats Who?

grass

goat

Bedouin drinks goat's milk

5

From chains to webs

A food chain shows how one animal eats one type of plant, or one other animal. But in the desert, where there might be little food, most animals have to eat whatever they can find. This means they depend on lots of different plants and animals – a relationship called a food web.

Houbara bustard

A food web in action

A food web shows how different food chains are connected. For example, the houbara bustard, which lives in the deserts of Central Asia, is part of many different food chains. This is because it eats plant seeds and shoots as well as locusts, beetles and lizards.

All these animals can be linked together in a food web. If the bustard could not find seeds, it might eat more beetles. This would leave fewer beetles for animals in other food chains to eat.

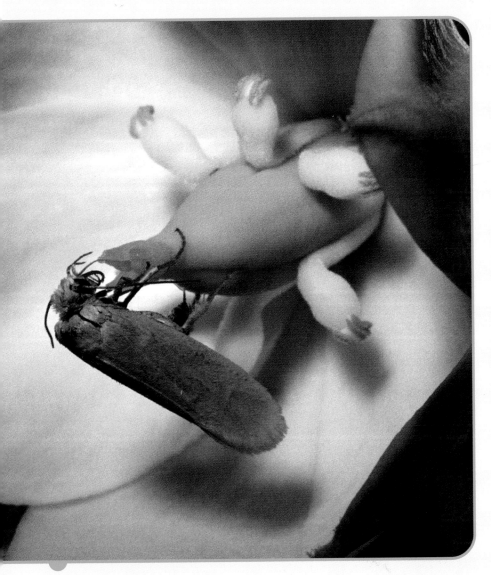
A desert yucca moth perches on a yucca flower.

Wet and dry webs

Weather has a great effect on food chains and food webs in the desert. In very dry weather, a lizard might eat seeds or small insects. When rain does finally arrive, plants burst into life and grow. Animals breed or travel into the desert to look for food, which gives the lizard more choice in what it eats.

Fussy eaters

Most desert animals eat whatever they can. However, some creatures are fussy. In the deserts of the USA, for example, the yucca moth only eats the yucca plant; the female moth lays its eggs on the plant. But the yucca plant depends on the yucca moth, too. Every time the female visits a yucca plant it spreads pollen from one yucca to another. This allows the yucca plant to reproduce.

Desert plants

Plants are the first link in any food chain, since they make their energy directly from sunlight through photosynthesis. This energy is available to other living things higher up the food chain.

Strong sunlight

Unlike plants elsewhere, desert plants face a unique problem – too much sunlight! In strong sunlight people often wear light-coloured clothes that reflect the sun and keep them cool. Many desert plants use the same idea. They have pale green or grey stems and branches to reflect the sunlight.

Ephemeral plants

Some plants, called ephemerals, spend most of the time lying in the ground as seeds. When it rains, the seeds burst into life, producing leaves in as little as two hours.

The plants flower briefly, then die, leaving more seeds to lie in wait for the next rains. Ephemerals can produce 1.5 billion seeds per hectare of desert!

Desert in bloom after rain, South Africa.

We're in the chain!

The San people, who live in Africa's Kalahari Desert, eat wild watermelons and cucumbers. The plants are an important source of water and vitamin C.

Yummy!

When ephemeral plants blossom after rain, honey ants feed some of their workers plant nectar until their bodies swell up. The other ants use the swollen workers as food containers, and suck the nectar from them. Honey ants are eaten by lizards, who are in turn eaten by birds of prey, such as hawks.

This huge saguaro cactus grows in the south-western USA.

Perennial plants

Plants that stay alive all the time are called perennials. Desert perennials include tough grasses. In very dry times the grasses look dead but their long roots are still alive under the ground. Other perennials are cactus plants, which grow in North and South America. After it has rained, cacti can store huge amounts of water in their stems, which swell like balloons.

Who Eats Who?

prickly pear (fruit)

worker honey ant

other honey ants eat nectar stored in worker

horned lizard

hawk

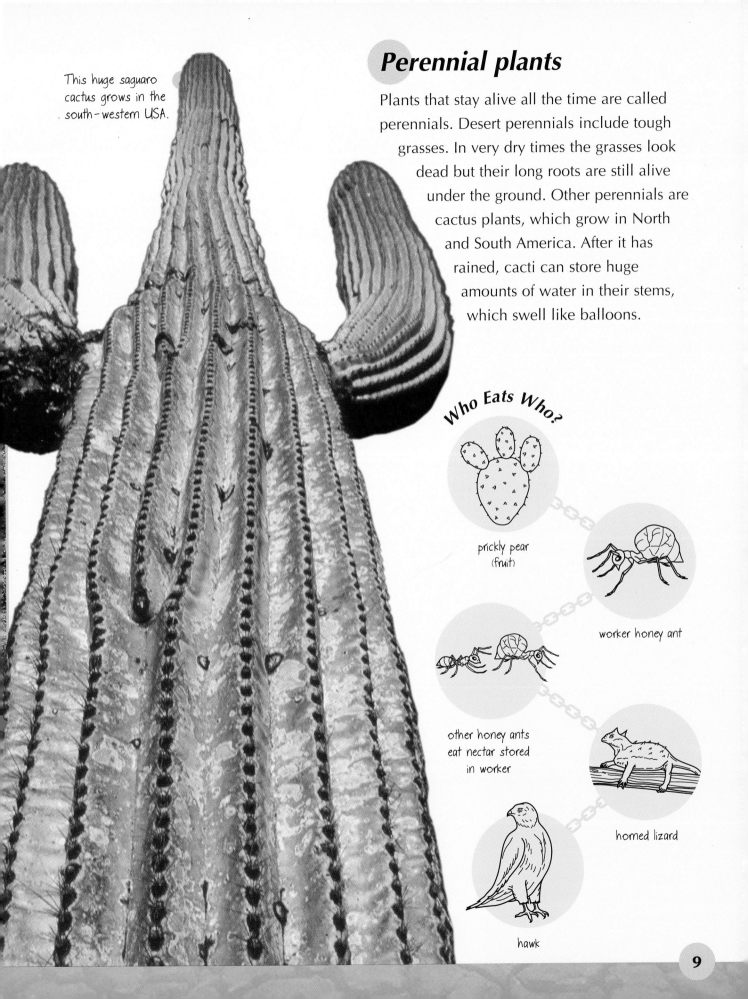

9

Eating it up

The first animal in a food chain is always a herbivore – a plant-eater. Herbivores in the desert range in size from tiny insects to big mammals, such as antelopes and kangaroos.

Small animal food chains

A female kangaroo and her baby, called a joey.

In the driest deserts there are few plants, so herbivores have to eat seeds or bits of plants blown into the desert on the wind. Deserts like this only have enough food for tiny plant-eaters, like insects.

The next animals in food chains are carnivores – meat-eaters. In very dry deserts the carnivores are small spiders or lizards, or small rodents. Other carnivores, such as snakes and birds, eat these animals.

Bigger animal food chains

Deserts with more plant life support larger herbivores. In Africa, deer-like mammals called gazelles get all the food and water they need from desert plants – some species spend their entire lives without drinking water.

Bigger herbivores attract bigger carnivores. Desert animals that hunt gazelles are jackals, hyenas and wild cats called caracals, which have short tails and pointed, tufty ears.

This wily coyote of the south-western USA is an omnivore – it has a varied diet.

Omnivores

Many desert animals are not purely herbivores or carnivores but omnivores – they eat everything! In the Mojave Desert in the USA, wild dogs called coyotes eat rabbits, rodents, antelopes and goats. But they are also happy to eat plants, especially the seed pods of the mesquite tree.

Breaking it down

When a living thing produces waste or dies, animals called decomposers break it down. The broken-down matter then provides nutrients that help plants to grow.

About decomposers

When a plant or animal dies, many animals will not eat it. But micro-organisms such as bacteria and fungi, known as decomposers, attack the dead matter. They eat it and begin to break it down.

In the desert, decomposers include beetles, earthworms and millipedes. These animals feed on dead and decaying bits of plants or animals that they find on or underneath the surface of the desert.

We're in the chain!

In Africa, people fry or roast winged termites, or grind them into a flour. Queen termites, in particular, are considered to be a delicacy.

A termite nest

Termites

Some of the most important desert decomposers are small insects with soft, pale bodies called termites. They look like ants, but are more closely related to cockroaches.

Most termites live underground in groups, called colonies, and eat a variety of dead material. Australian scientists have found that desert termites there eat dead grasses, leaves, roots and wood, and sheep and kangaroo dung.

Smaller decomposers

After beetles, earthworms and termites have eaten the dead plant or animal material, most of it passes out of their bodies into the soil. But now it is in much smaller pieces, ready for even tinier animals to eat.

These micro-organisms include nematode worms and protozoans, which can be less than 0.01 mm long. These decomposers break down this waste, releasing minerals that help new plants grow.

Who Eats Who?

camel dung

scarab beetle

termite (eats beetle's waste)

nematode worm (eats termite's waste)

new plant (helped to grow by minerals released by broken down dung)

Yummy!

African dung beetles gather up the dung of animals, such as camels and goats, and roll it into balls. The beetle buries the ball underground and later feeds off it.

Dung beetle

The desert at night

When the temperature drops at night the desert comes alive with activity. Many animals emerge to look for seeds, nibble at plants or hunt other creatures.

The fennec fox

In the Sahara Desert lives a small mammal weighing less than a pet cat. It is a type of fox called a fennec (right) and it comes out at night to catch lizards, insects and rodents such as gerbils.

The fennec is well adapted to night-time hunting. It has a good sense of smell and huge ears that pick up the tiniest noises of its prey. During the day, the fennec's big ears also help its body heat to escape.

Keeping cool

Mammals are warm-blooded. This means their bodies always stay at the same temperature. Most desert mammals, including rodents, rabbits, foxes and cats, are nocturnal – they are active at night.

The reason for this is that warm-blooded mammals feel comfortable in the chilly desert night, but they can overheat during the day. To avoid this, many animals spend the daytime sleeping in cool underground burrows or beneath rocks.

An angry scorpion holds its tail up, ready to strike.

Yummy!

The ningaui is a tiny rodent that lives in Australia's deserts. It weighs only 4 g, but is an aggressive night hunter. The ningaui's two favourite meals – desert centipedes and cockroaches – are bigger than it is!

Insects, spiders and scorpions

Many smaller desert creatures like flies, ants and grasshoppers, as well as spiders, are also active at night. Scorpions can survive fiercer heat than insects, but they too are nocturnal.

Some scorpions are 12 cm long. They are bold hunters and catch spiders, insects and other scorpions with their powerful pincers, before killing them with the poison stings in their tails. The poison from some scorpions is so strong that it can kill a person in a few hours.

Daytime desert

Daytime desert food chains are made up of animals whose bodies can withstand the scorching, dry heat.

Reptiles rule

The kings of the daytime desert – lizards, snakes and tortoises – are reptiles. Unlike mammals, reptiles are cold-blooded. Their body temperature changes according to their surroundings.

At night, when desert temperatures drop, reptiles lose their body heat and have little energy for hunting. In daytime, however, the heat of the sun warms them up, giving them the energy to look for food.

A blazing daytime desert scene.

Western diamondback rattlesnake

16

Lizards and tortoises

The largest lizard of all is the desert monitor lizard. It lives in Africa and Asia and grows to 1.6 m. A much smaller lizard is the spiny-tailed lizard of northern Africa, which reaches about 30 cm.

Most lizards and snakes (see pages 18-19) are carnivores, but tortoises are herbivores. The desert tortoise of the USA can store nearly a litre of water in its body just from the plants it eats, and survives on this liquid during dry times.

Spiny-tailed lizard

Yummy!

The Egyptian spiny-tailed lizard likes to eat both plant matter and insects, such as crickets. Its armoured tail keeps predators away.

We're in the chain!

Although their traditional ways are becoming much less common, some San people in the Kalahari Desert still hunt animals such as antelope using bows and poisoned arrows, as well as with animal traps.

Daytime mammals

Not all desert mammals come out at night. Many large mammals cope with the heat better than smaller ones and some, like antelopes, camels and kangaroos, are too big to find shelter from the sun.

Antelopes, for example, can withstand increases in their body temperature even though they are warm-blooded. And a camels' thick fur coat actually acts as a shield against the sun.

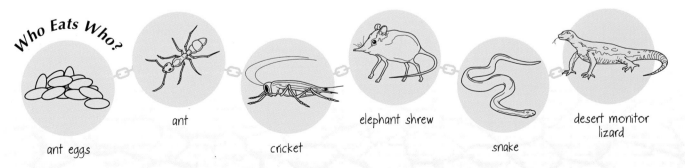

Who Eats Who?

ant eggs

ant

cricket

elephant shrew

snake

desert monitor lizard

Life in the sand

Sandy desert regions provide animals with a cool place to burrow and hide from the sun. But the sand is not always safe – expert hunters are never far away.

Small sand-dwellers

Smaller creatures that live in the sand include camel crickets, scorpions, beetles, cockroaches and spiders. These animals don't burrow just for the cooler temperatures there, but because they know they may be able to find water beneath the surface, or the remains of plant or animal matter. One fearsome insect that hunts in the sand is the larva of the antlion fly. It digs a pit in the sand, covers itself with more sand and waits for another insect to slide down into the hole and then eats it.

Antlion fly lava

Young bearded
dragon lizard

Bigger sand-dwellers

A bigger animal that eats insects that burrow in the sand is the legless skink lizard of Africa's Namib Desert. The skink moves through the sand by wriggling. It once had legs but has lost them through evolution.

In Australia, the bearded dragon lizard grows to about 50 cm. It is an expert hunter, eating all kinds of smaller sand-dwelling creatures.

Snakes

Many snakes are also very good at hunting in the sand but they move across the surface rather than burrowing into it. Sidewinding snakes move by slithering sideways.

The sidewinding adder of the Namib Desert plays a hunting trick. The only part of the snake's body visible above the sand is its tail. It moves its tail to imitate an insect and so attracts unwary lizards.

Life on a plant

Some desert plants are a home to many different animals and contain entire food chains.
This is especially true of the saguaro cactus and the desert ironwood tree, both found in the deserts of the south-western USA.

Saguaro cactus

The saguaro cactus is the tallest of all cactus plants, growing up to 15 m in height. Despite its poisonous, prickly spines, many animals live on or in the saguaro.

Desert woodpeckers make holes in the top of the plant, in which they build nests. Cactus pygmy owls, which are small enough to fit into a person's hand, often move into these nests when woodpeckers have left. The owls hunt other birds, lizards, rodents and insects that live on or near the cactus.

This desert woodpecker nests in a saguaro cactus.

We're in the chain!

Native Americans have traditionally ground up the seeds of the desert ironwood tree and eaten them. They have also used the tree's flowers and roots for medicines.

Yummy!

Cactus pygmy owls kill and eat other birds, such as doves, which can be more than twice their own size.

A cactus pygmy owl and its chicks in their nest in the middle of a saguaro cactus.

Ironwood chain

Desert ironwood trees support around 500 plant and animal species in their native region of the USA's Sonoran Desert. The ironwood's leaves give shade to many creatures. Most years the tree produces hard seed pods, which rodents such as the kangaroo rat like to break open and eat. Kangaroo rats are eaten in their turn by long-nosed snakes, and snakes by kit foxes and other larger mammals.

Helping other plants

The desert ironwood also offers shade to smaller plants, such as cacti and wild flowers, and protects them from cold temperatures at night. The plants that grow underneath ironwoods attract more animals to feed there, including jack rabbits, desert bighorn sheep and deer.

Who Eats Who?

ironwood seeds

kangaroo rat

long-nosed snake

kit fox

21

From the ground to the air

Birds and flying insects have a big advantage over other desert animals. They can travel farther to hunt whatever food is available.

Desert birds

In Australia, desert birds include brightly-coloured parrots as well as the Australian bustard, which grabs lizards and rodents with its sharp beak and swallows them whole. The roadrunner of the south-western USA (right) prefers to walk rather than fly. It eats insects, scorpions, lizards and even rattlesnakes.

In Africa and the USA, two large birds that often fly over deserts are the golden eagle and the vulture. All eagles kill their own prey, but vultures are scavengers so they look for animals that are dead already.

Locusts gather together in huge swarms.

Cooling down

Because flying creates a lot of heat, birds are used to high body temperatures. Their feathers provide protection from the sun's rays, and many birds also cool down by fluttering the skin on their throats – just like we use a fan.

Yummy!

The female Namib wasp paralyzes a spider with its sting, before laying an egg on it. When the egg hatches, the wasp larva eats the spider for its first meal.

Locusts

Insects, such as flies, wasps, crickets and butterflies also fly over the desert. But the best-known flying desert insects are locusts. Locusts fly together in huge groups, or swarms, of up to 40 billion.

As they fly, locusts are pulled by low air pressure to places where it has rained and plants are growing. Swarms can eat up all the plants in an area of desert. This can seriously affect food chains and webs for other animals and ruin farm crops.

Reptile snack: a roadrunner devours a lizard.

A watery food chain

Rain showers in the desert cause new life to burst out, and trigger off short-lived food chains. One of these chains involves the amazing spadefoot toad of the Arizona Desert in the USA.

Spadefoot toads

Most toads like damp places, so they are not natural desert dwellers. The spadefoot toad is different. It hides in a burrow that it digs under the ground with its hind feet.

After a rare desert rain shower, the spadefoot emerges into daylight. Male and female toads mate, and the female lays her eggs in a shallow pool that the rain has made.

Race for survival

As soon as the eggs hatch into tadpoles, the race begins for them to grow into adults before their watery home in the pool dries up. This is because an adult toad can live out of water, but a tadpole cannot.

The pools are full of algae, water fleas and tiny shrimp that come to life when it rains. All are food for the tadpoles.

Spadefoot toad

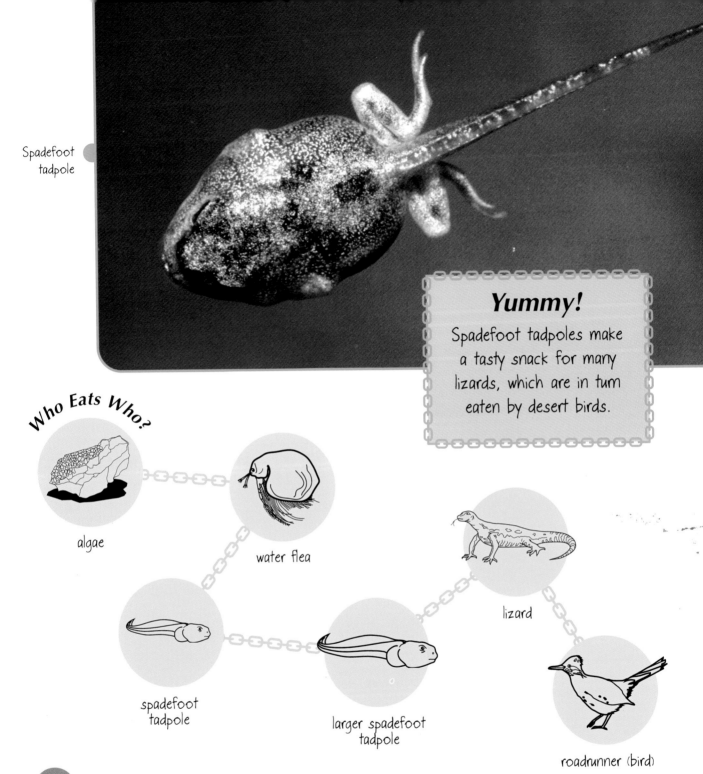

Spadefoot tadpole

Who Eats Who?

algae

water flea

lizard

spadefoot tadpole

larger spadefoot tadpole

roadrunner (bird)

Tadpoles eating tadpoles

The pools can also contain larger shrimps called fairy shrimp. If there are fairy shrimp around, some tadpoles develop bigger heads and mouths to eat them. And the bigger tadpoles don't stop there – they also start to eat the smaller tadpoles too. This means the bigger tadpoles can become toads even more quickly, which might be vital if the pool is fast drying out.

On the edge of the desert

Many deserts are surrounded by grasslands or mountains. While these areas are still hot and dry, they receive more rain than deserts themselves and so attract more plants and animals.

Savannah

On the edge of many deserts lies a region of grasses and scattered trees known as savannah. In Africa, herds of antelope and gazelle often roam this region. But they must stay on the alert for the animals that hunt them, such as lions, leopards, cheetahs and caracals.

Lion

We're in the chain!

As people build more homes and cities on the edge of deserts, so animals adapt to their new surroundings. In cities on the edge of deserts in the south-western USA, for example, coyotes often eat scraps of food from rubbish bins.

Staying together

Many antelopes and gazelles stay in large herds for safety. Most young antelope are born around the same time for the same reason. If they were born throughout the year the big cats would have a constant supply of vulnerable prey.

Many antelope wander deep into the desert, for example after rains, when more plants grow. At such times, lions and other predators follow them, in search of a meal.

Rare rhinoceroses

The region around the Namib Desert in south-west Africa has both flat savannah and high mountains. It is home to many endangered animals, such as the mountain zebra and the black rhinoceros. Like the zebra, the rhinoceros is a herbivore, feeding on grasses and woody plants. Rhinoceroses have few predators – apart from people, who have killed them in large numbers for their horns.

Who Eats Who?

leaf

springbok (antelope)

leopard

A springbok in a South African desert setting.

Yummy!

Birds such as oxpeckers spend a lot of their time on rhinoceroses' backs, eating the small insects that make their home there.

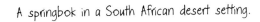

Food web

Here is a typical desert food web, together with some fascinating desert facts.

Deserts and semi-deserts make up nearly one-third of the Earth's land area.

Some desert animals, including fennec foxes and certain scorpions, obtain all the water they need from the animals they kill.

Tortoises

Decomposers
(bacteria and fungi, insects and earthworms, protozoans and nematode worms)

Desert plants
(perennials and ephemerals)

Insects

Herbivores, mammals and birds

To find water deep underground, the roots of the camelthom acacia tree, which grows in African deserts, can reach down 30 m.

The hottest air temperature ever recorded was in the Sahara Desert in Libya in 1922. It was 57.8°C.

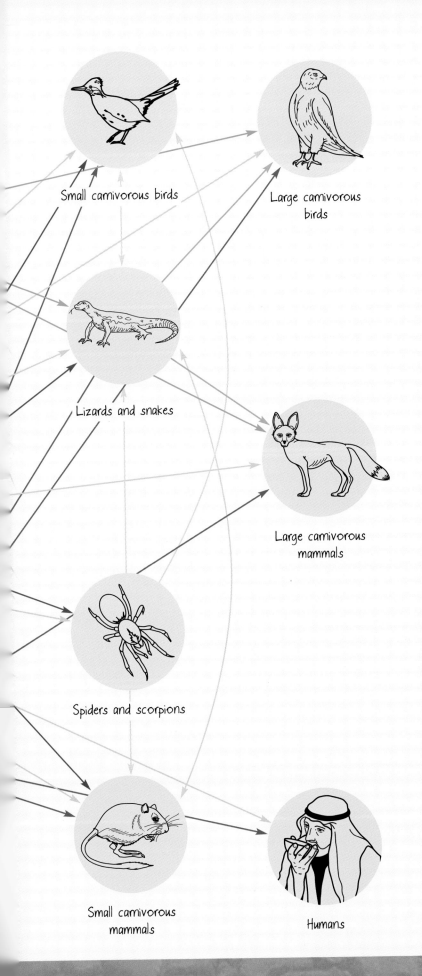

Small carnivorous birds

Large carnivorous birds

Lizards and snakes

Large carnivorous mammals

Spiders and scorpions

Small carnivorous mammals

Humans

The date palm tree is a very important plant for people living in the deserts of North Africa and the Middle East. They eat its fruit (dates), use the wood for houses and the leaves for fences, baskets and sandals.

Fairy shrimp eggs can blow with the desert dust for 50 years before rains cause the shrimp to hatch and grow.

Some bristlecone pine trees, which grow in the deserts of North America, have been alive for about 5,000 years.

Scientists think there are around 1,200 different types of plant in the Sahara Desert and about 40 different kinds of rodent!

Glossary

algae

very simple types of plants that do not have stems, roots or leaves. Most algae live in watery places, but some live in deserts.

bacteria

tiny, one-celled micro-organisms that live in soil, as well as in water, plants and animals' bodies.

carnivore

a meat-eating animal.

cold-blooded

an animal whose body temperature is linked to the outside temperature. At night, when it is cold, cold-blooded animals are also cold. When the sun rises, they warm up. Insects, spiders, fish, amphibians and reptiles are all cold-blooded.

decomposer

a living thing that feeds on and breaks down dead plants and animals as well as animal waste.

desert

a region with few plants and trees, where it rarely rains. One definition of a desert is a place that receives less than 25 cm of rain each year.

ephemerals

plants that live for a very short time. In the desert, ephemeral plants remain lifeless as seeds until it rains. They quickly sprout roots, flower and produce seeds.

fungus

a type of organism (the plural is "fungi") that lives on dead or rotting things. Mould, mushrooms and rust are all types of fungus.

herbivore

a plant-eating animal.

larva (pl. larvae)

the form that an insect takes when it hatches from an egg. Larvae often look very different from adult insects.

micro-organism

a living thing that is so small it can only be seen under a microscope.

nectar

a sweet, sticky liquid that plants produce. Bees use nectar to make honey.

nocturnal

describes an animal that comes out at night to eat and perform other activities, such as hunting.

nomad

a member of a group of people who move their home from place to place, in search of good land on which their herds of animals can feed.

omnivore

an animal that eats plants and other animals. Many desert animals are omnivores.

perennials

plants that survive all year round, and sometimes for many, many years. Some desert perennial plants are around 5,000 years old.

photosynthesis

the process by which plants capture the energy of sunlight to make sugar.

pollen

tiny, dust-like specks in a flower that make plant seeds grow.

predator

an animal that kills and eats other animals.

savannah

an area of grassland that contains scattered trees or bushes. Some savannah regions are on the edge of deserts.

scavenger

an animal that eats dead or dying things. Decomposers are scavengers, but the best-known are vultures.

warm-blooded

animals that maintain the same body temperature when it is hot or cold outside.

Desert websites

www.oxfam.org.uk/coolplanet/ontheline/explore/nature/deserts/deserts.htm
Informative site – a collaboration between Oxfam UK, WWF-UK and Channel 4.

www.ucmp.berkeley.edu/glossary/gloss5/biome/deserts.html
All about deserts, from the University of California at Berkeley.

http://digital-desert.com/wildlife/
Lots of good information about US desert wildlife.

Index